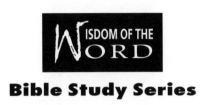

Bible Study Series

Ezra
Leader of Moral Restoration

Linda Shaw

BEACON HILL PRESS
OF KANSAS CITY

KANSAS CITY, MISSOURI

Copyright 1999

by Beacon Hill Press of Kansas City

ISBN 083-411-8017

Printed in the United States of America

Cover Design: Marie Tabler

10   9   8   7   6   5   4   3   2   1

Contents

Introduction to Ezra

L E S S O N   1

L E S S O N   2

L E S S O N   3

L E S S O N   4

L E S S O N   5

L E S S O N   6

L E S S O N   7

L E S S O N   8

L E S S O N   9

L E S S O N   1 0

Introduction to Ezra

The Chinese hieroglyphic figure for "crisis" could be translated into both "danger" and "opportunity." Certainly the children of Israel were once again in crisis; they were not a free people able to serve their God as He would desire. Instead, they were captives in a foreign land exposed to all sorts of evil and foreign religions. One of the true dangers was that many of them had become comfortable in their captivity and could no longer recognize that they were in danger of losing their very souls; therefore, they could not be a chosen people set apart to represent the holiness of God.

Then opportunity knocked at the door in the form of Cyrus. As we read the book of Ezra, we discover that the Neo-Babylonian Empire has just been overthrown by Cyrus the Persian. He was an enlightened king who did not believe in repressive measures and, therefore, displayed some restraint toward those he had conquered. Citizens forcibly removed from their homeland were free to return. Religious tolerance was Cyrus's forte. He appointed Darius the Mede to rule the Babylonian territory, and he subsequently placed God's servant Daniel in a position of honor (Daniel 5:30—6:3).

So Cyrus represents "opportunity," for he would let God's people go. They were free to go back to their homeland and fulfill God's promise to them if they showed courage. They would have to leave "the comfort of their captivity" and face more dangers in new, unsettled land, but God would supply all their needs *according to his riches in glory* (Philippians 4:19, KJV).

The Old Testament prophets had warned Israel of Babylonian exile if they were not obedient to

God's laws. Jeremiah specifically prophesied 70 years of captivity (Jeremiah 24:11-12). Babylon fell to Persia in 539 B.C. through God's use of Cyrus (Isaiah 45:15). Then the opportunity for return to the homeland became possible. Jeremiah also prophesied the first and second return of the Jews to Israel in Jeremiah 25:11 and 29:10.

In the book of Ezra, two sets of exiles return. The first set returned during the time of Zerubbabel and Sheshbazzar, which is covered in chapters 1—6 (the return for Babylon, Ezra 1 and 2; the Temple construction initiated, Ezra 3 and 4; and the Temple construction completed, Ezra 5 and 6). The second section of the book deals with the return of exiles during the time of Ezra's leadership. This is covered in Ezra 7—10 (the return to Jerusalem in chapters 7—8 and reformation of the people in chapters 9—10). Between the two sections there is a gap of 60 years.

Ezra, whose name means "help," is most likely the author of both Ezra and Nehemiah, which may have originally been written as one book. They are part of three historical books called the

---

As you begin each day, use this acrostic to help you study:

Wait for the Holy Spirit to teach you as you read His Word.

Obey what God instructs you to do.

Remember to praise God for insights and promises fulfilled.

Discover for yourself the incredible faithfulness of God!

"Postcaptivity" that also includes Esther. They were probably written around 450-430 B.C. Ezra was a descendant of Zadok and Phinehas and therefore, fell into the line of priest. However, in captivity Ezra had no place to serve as priest, for there was no Temple. He gave himself over to studying the law of Moses and became a skilled scribe. He has been credited with organizing the synagogue and being the founder of the order of scribes. He is said to have arranged the Psalms, and he probably wrote Psalm 119. It is also possible that he wrote 1 and 2 Chronicles.

Ezra was commissioned by the king to go to Jerusalem to inquire into the civil and religious condition of the Jewish community. When he did so, he took 1700 to 2000 exiles with him. Upon his return, he initiated a new era in which the Pentateuch was not only a book of law but an instruction manual for living. Ezra became the father of Judaism and this new way of life.

In Ezra 7:10, we see that Ezra set his heart to study, practice, and teach the Law of the Lord. The Word would have to change the people. Just as we need to do today, Ezra emphasized the *word of the Lord* (Ezra 1:1, 3:2, 6:14, 18; 7:6, 10, 14; 9:4; 10:3, 5) The people listened and *trembled at the words of the God of Israel* (Ezra 9:4 and 10:3)

The theme of the book of Ezra is God's faithfulness to fulfill His promises to His people. He warned them of captivity due to disobedience, but He also gave them hope of restoration and led them back to their promised land. There is also the subtheme of Satan's strategies as he worked to sabotage the building of the Temple and instill discouragement and fear into the people. Another subtheme is the separation from sin that God's people must display. The Israelites were to be a holy people, set apart. They were not to become involved with foreign gods or ways that were contrary to God's laws.

So the challenge begins. With crisis comes challenge, and with challenge comes danger and opportunity. How will God's people fare? Will they have the courage to face the challenge and conquer foes in His name?

As we begin the study of Ezra, we also are challenged by danger and opportunity. Will we read God's words but allow them to blow away like chaff in the wind? We are blessed with His Word and the opportunity to grow in His Spirit, but that is always a challenge for it requires time and energy and work. May we, like Ezra, rise to the occasion to please God, our Lord and King.

Ezra

■ A study of Ezra 1

DAY ONE

Proper Places

Read Ezra 1, concentrating on verse 1.

Because they had disobeyed God, His people found themselves living in Babylon instead of the Promised Land. Prophets had come forth to call the Israelites back to God's laws, but the Old Testament tells us that they were a stiff-necked people who refused to obey. Just as they had ended up as slaves in Egypt, they became captives in Babylon under Nebuchadnezzar. Seventy years had passed, and Babylon had fallen to the Medes and Persians. The ruler of the new kingdom was Cyrus.

Cyrus reigned from 559 to 530 B.C. However, he was not in power in Babylon until around 539 B.C., when he conquered this area. His philosophy about captured peoples was totally different from Nebuchadnezzar's philosophy.

Nebuchadnezzar held the traditional view that because the most powerful kingdom always conquered, the god of that kingdom must be the most powerful. So as he conquered most of the known world, he collected those weaker gods, destroyed their temples, and brought the gods to the temple of his god in Babylon. As a result, Nebuchadnezzar's kingdom was full of foreign gods.

Cyrus, on the other hand, was a believer in many gods. He believed his gods would smile on him if he put all the idols back in their proper places. So as one of his first public acts, he ordered displaced people to be allowed to return to their homelands to rebuild their temples and put their gods back in place. Cyrus even hoped that worship would be reestablished and he would receive a blessing.

A story appeared in a newspaper recently about a junior high girl named Barbara who one day in the

1950s decided to skip school to meet her friend at the Oklahoma City Golf and Country Club. She rode the city bus to the slightly familiar location, got out and entered the lobby. Her friend had not yet arrived, so she sat down to wait. When a man approached and asked if he could help her, she replied that she was waiting for a friend. A few minutes later, another man appeared and asked the same question. When Barbara gave the same reply, he asked her if she knew where she was. The startled young girl queried, "This is the Oklahoma City Golf and Country Club, isn't it?" "Oh, no," the man smiled, "this is my home." Barbara, embarrassed, apologized profusely, but the kind man simply summoned his chauffeur and had her driven to the proper place.

Cyrus also was unruffled about helping others find their proper places. He quickly learned how to win the favor of those he conquered. By allowing them to return to their homelands and practice their religions, he sealed his popularity and throne. His people lovingly called him the "father" of their nation because he worshiped their gods, including those of Babylonia and Israel.

The fact that Cyrus desired to return the gods to their proper places might make it easy to credit him with being a God-worshiper. He was actually a "polytheist" since he did not acknowledge God as the

MEMORY CHALLENGE

Psalm 37:1

Do not fret because of evil men or be envious of those who do wrong.

(NIV)

one and only true God. God refers to Cyrus when stating, *For the sake of Jacob my servant, of Israel my chosen, I summon you by name and bestow on you a title of honor, though you do not acknowledge me* (Isaiah 45:4). Could it be that in spite of the fact that Cyrus was not a follower of the God of Abraham, Isaac, and Jacob, God used him anyway?

1. Read Philippians 2:13. Write out this scripture and explain how it relates to Cyrus.

2. What does one's purposes have to do with his proper place? After answering, examine the proper place of Ruth, Esther, and Jonah.

   Ruth 1:14-18

   Esther 4:12-17

   Jonah 3:1-10

3. Do you know your proper place in God's plan? If you do, are you keeping it as a priority in your life? List your priorities below to help serve as a reminder.

   Priorities

   1.

   2.

   3.

   4.

   5.

   6.

4. If you do not know your proper place, are you seeking God's face to discover His plan? Read and summarize the following scriptures as a start:

   Psalm 119:10-11

   Proverbs 3:4-5

   Isaiah 48:17

   Psalm 32:8

Prophecy

Read Ezra 1:1 and Isaiah 44:28—45:1, 13.

1. List the major points of the prophecies of Isaiah, written of Cyrus and Jerusalem 200 years before actual events occurred.

2. Using a dictionary or Bible concordance, write out the definition of the word "prophecy."

3. What portion of Ezra 1:1 relates to prophecy?

4. Read Jeremiah 25:11-12 and record the major points.

Prophecy always involved an element of revealing God's will to a people or nation. It was often a call to correction in order to avoid the consequences of disobedience. Occasionally there were warnings of future events if God's laws and plan were not followed. It was a message from God to His people through a human instrument.

For the "instrument" there were no personal issues at stake; it wasn't even popular to be a prophet. It was simply the prophet's role to reveal the message of God that often the people did not want to hear. They could become angry at the "instrument" God used, often persecuting him mercilessly.

Many of the prophecies of the Bible have been fulfilled although others are yet to be. But prophecy itself stands as a mark of authenticity of God's Word; many events prophesied hundreds of years before their occurrence were indeed completed in history just as foretold by the prophets. Cyrus is an example of this as he was named in scripture 200 years before he was born. Jeremiah prophesied that he would be used of God to let the Jews return to their homeland.

Cyrus appointed Darius to rule the Babylonian Empire in his stead because he lived at his home in Persia. This is recorded in Daniel 5:30, since these events were taking place during Daniel's captivity. In Daniel 9, a story is related from this era. *In the first year of Darius son of Xerxes (a Mede by descent), who was made ruler over the Babylonian kingdom—in the first year of his reign, I, Daniel, understood from the Scriptures, according to the Word of the LORD given to Jeremiah the prophet, that the desolation of Jerusalem would last seventy years. So I turned to the Lord God and pleaded with him in prayer and petition, in fasting, and in sackcloth and ashes* (Daniel 9:1-3). So it was the reading of the prophecy of Jeremiah that caused Daniel to pray.

Should we worry over evil men?

Proclamation

Read Ezra 1:2-4.

1. Whom did Cyrus credit with giving him all the kingdoms of the earth?

2. What did Cyrus believe God had appointed him to do?

3. What did Cyrus give God's people permission to do?

4. Those of God's people who did not return to Jerusalem were to do what?

5. What do you think this proclamation has to do with proper places?

6. How does 2 Chronicles 36:22-23 relate to the background information and proclamation?

On January 1, 1863, the most important proclamation in American history was released by Abraham Lincoln. Lincoln told Francis B. Carpenter, his portrait painter, that it was "the central act of my administration and the greatest event of the 19th century." Of course, this was the Emancipation Proclamation, which announced that slavery would no longer be legal in the United States of America. Up to this point the purpose of the war had been to stop the expansion of slavery, but now the forces shifted to freedom for all slaves. This proclamation further polarized the North and South but gave life to the concept of life, liberty, freedom, and equality to all people in the United States, a principle upon which the nation had originally been established. Real freedom did not come until the war was over, and the United States Congress passed the 13th amendment making all people free. But the Emancipation Proclamation started the process and made the intentions of the North very clear.

Proclamations or announcements are also found in the Bible. Isaiah 61:1-2 states that Isaiah is to proclaim freedom for the captives and the year of the Lord's favor. John the Baptist saw Jesus coming toward him and proclaimed, *Look, the Lamb of God, who takes away the sin of the world!* (John 1:29). Revelation 5:2 tells us that an angel proclaimed the worthiness of the Lion of Judah. But formal announcements like the Emancipation Proclamation, an executive notice issued under the authority of the head of state announcing an order important to the subject, were rare. Yet Cyrus made a major proclamation of permission and duty. He announced freedom for the Jews who desired to return to their homeland to rebuild the Temple and establish their former ways of life and religion.

We should not be envious of whom?

Preparation

Read Ezra 1:5 and Ephesians 6:10-18.

In Girl Scouts, one of the first things learned is the motto, "Be prepared." One Girl Scout fondly recounted how her troop learned to be prepared: "We wrote up menus and developed grocery lists. We recorded needed camping items and collected our gear. We scheduled our daily activities and sometimes even created special equipment for the activities. I remember a little oven we made from directions in the Girl Scout guide. When we finished it, we took it with us on a trip, using it to bake little cakes. To a Girl Scout, 'Be Prepared' was no idle motto, but one to be taken seriously."

The heads of the families who determined to go to Jerusalem and build God's Temple also had to be prepared. Cyrus had made some provisions for them in his proclamation, but God was to be the One who would really keep them prepared. As each problem arose, the answer was found in the providence of God when His people came to Him. They could not be totally prepared for the actual circumstances, but they could be mentally, emotionally, and spiritually prepared for what would come by seeking God's face.

We, too, must be prepared for the problems that will come our way, for the reality in this world is that we will have tribulation (John 16:33). We are not to be naive (for that makes us easy prey for Satan) but knowledgeable regarding life, including evil, so we can fight the schemes of the devil. God always makes provisions for us and has given us a way to be prepared.

1. Why do we need to be prepared with the full armor of God? (See Ephesians 6:11.)

2. Who inspires the struggles that we face in life (Ephesians 6:12)? Was it any different for the people of Ezra's day?

3. Why do we put on the armor of God? (See Ephesians 6:13.)

4. Match the armor of God with its meaning below:

Belt	Salvation
Breastplate	Word of God
Feet	Righteousness
Helmet	Truth
Shield	Readiness with gospel of peace
Sword	Faith

5. How are we to pray in order to be prepared?

6. Name the phrase in verse 18 that is similar to "Be prepared" and explain how the two relate to each other.

MEMORY CHALLENGE

"Do not _____ because of _____ _____ or be _____ of those who do _____."

Psalm _____:1

People

Read Ezra 1:6-8.

1. Who are the four people specifically named in these verses?

2. These four people represent those used in God's plan to accomplish His purposes. People in our lives are important also. Name two people who have been important in your journey with God, and state why each of them is important.

3. Write in the blanks below how the person on the left was important to the person on the right.

   Aaron _____ Moses
   (Exodus 4:10-17)

   Elisha _____ Elijah
   (1 Kings 19:19-21)

   Timothy _____ Paul
   (1 Timothy 1:1-2)

4. From your study of the Word, choose a Bible character who has influenced your life.

5. As a follower of Christ, your witness is important to many others. Name one or two people upon whom you feel you have a spiritual impact. If you do not feel you are serving others in this way at all, write a prayer to God about it here.

One way of being prepared for the journey so that we can fulfill God's purpose is to surround ourselves with godly people who will encourage us to be godly. If we surround ourselves with unrighteous people, they will encourage our own unrighteousness. We need holy people in our lives for love, support, wisdom, encouragement, and accountability. As we mature in the faith, we are to pass this on to others and be their godly influence.

One interesting and mysterious person in this passage is Sheshbazzar. By Ezra 3, the man in this position seems to be called Zerubbabel. What is the confusion? Theologians give us three views:

The first view is that both are the same person, but one is his Babylonian or Persian name and one is his Hebrew name. Daniel and his friends—Hannaniah, Mishael, and Azariah—also experienced this cultural name change. After being taken into Babylonian captivity, they were called Belteshazzar, Shadrach, Meshach, and Abednego (Daniel 1:6-7). Possibly Sheshbazzar, or "joy in tribulation," was his name in captivity and Zerubbabel, or "stranger in Babylon," was his Hebrew name. He was the grandson of King Jehoiachin and ancestor of Joseph.

The second theory is that Sheshbazzar and Zerubbabel are two different people. Sheshbazzar was the official leader of the people and therefore received the articles from the Temple.

The third view is that Sheshbazzar was appointed by Cyrus but died soon after the return to Jerusalem, so his nephew Zerubbabel took over.

MEMORY CHALLENGE

Look for an opportunity this week to share with someone that he or she does not need to fear evil men.

Provision

Read Ezra 1:9-11.

1. Read Daniel 5:2-4. How did God's inventory of gold and silver utensils for the Temple get to Babylon? What were they used for there?

2. Now the utensils were being sent back by Cyrus as a way of providing for the exiles. How does God provide for us? Give an example.

3. Summarize the following verses regarding provisions.

   Genesis 22:6-8, 13

   Deuteronomy 31:8

   Psalm 65:9

   Matthew 10:9

   John 14:15-18

4. What are some nonmaterial ways in which God provides for us?

5. How does God use people as His instruments for these provisions?

When the exiles returned to Jerusalem, they did not go empty-handed. Just as God provided support for the Israelites when they left Egypt (Exodus 12:35-36), He provided for His children when they left Babylon. God made the Egyptians *favorably disposed toward the people,* and they were generous. Cyrus was generous because he believed he was returning the gods to the proper places.

Because God's people worshipped a live Deity that had no graven image, Nebuchadnazzar had taken the articles used in worship from the Temple in Jerusalem. This posed a problem for Cyrus in that he could not return the god to its proper place, so he returned these utensils. Since he wanted the people to resume their worship, he assumed these gold and silver articles would be needed.

The 5,400 vessels were probably only the *major* items. Smaller articles were likely neither counted nor recorded. So God, through Cyrus, was very generous. Also, those not actually returning to Jerusalem but wanting to participate offered gold and silver items (Ezra 1:6). God's people were not going back empty-handed but with abundant provisions.

MEMORY CHALLENGE

Practice by saying the verse aloud three times.

Ezra

LESSON 2

■ A study of Ezra 2

Lost Land

Read Ezra 2, concentrating on verse 1.

1. Summarize Genesis 12:1-3.

2. Did God fulfill this promise to Abraham? Check Acts 7:1-5 for the answer and additional information.

3. After Abraham came Isaac, Jacob, and his twelve sons who became the twelve tribes of Israel. They lived in the Promised Land but later moved. Why? (See Genesis 45:4-11.)

4. Once again God brought His people back to the Promised Land. Summarize Exodus 3:7-10 to learn the next step in the process.

5. Who was the actual person to take the Israelites into the Promised Land, and what did God say to him? (Joshua 1:1-8)

Psalm 37:2

For like the grass they will soon wither; like green plants they will soon die away.

(NIV)

6. The scripture from Question 5 gives a hint (verses 7-8) about why God's people are once again in captivity. What do you think is the reason?

7. Give some of the specifics of who carried whom into captivity as found in 2 Kings 24:14-16 and 2 Chronicles 36:20.

The Old Testament is the story of a people—the Israelites. God's plan was for them to be His people, set apart and obedient to Him. Abraham was called to a new land and answered that call in obedience and faith. His descendants were rewarded with Canaan or the "Promised Land." However, due to a famine they ended up in Egypt in the land of Goshen. But God delivered them to Canaan once again through Moses and Joshua. Through this period Israel became a powerful nation and could defend itself against any military enemy, for God was with His people and blessed them. But as they became more lax with God's law and more disobedient, they once again were overrun. This time they lost their land to Nebuchadnezzar, King of Babylon, who, as we studied in the last lesson, was overtaken by the Medes and Persians. But it was Nebuchadnezzar who actually took them captive and brought them to Babylon.

The book of Ezra marks the beginning of winning back the lost land. Unfortunately, the story does not end there. After Ezra's reign and the restoration, the people again became disobedient, even though God sent prophet after prophet to warn them of the requirement to follow His law. They refused to turn and be obedient and as a result were conquered by the Romans. Although this time they were not transported from their land, they did become an occupied people who could not run their own government or country. That is the situation we find Israel in when the Messiah, Jesus Christ, comes.

Disobedience is a condition of the heart that results not only in lost land, but lost dreams, lost insight, lost priorities, lost purpose, lost commitments, and lost love. In the end we can lose our very souls if we choose to disobey God's laws and reject His love. The writer of Hebrews states, *We must pay more careful attention, therefore, to what we have heard, so that we do not drift away. For if the message spoken by angels was binding, and every violation and disobedience received its just punishment, how shall we escape if we ignore such a great salvation?* (Hebrews 2:1-2).

It has been said that there are three types of people: foolish people who repeat their mistakes, knowledgeable people who learn from their mistakes, and wise people who learn from the mistakes of other people. The Israelites were not even knowledgeable, let alone wise. But we can be. We have lived through the 20th century, which gives us a good enough look back at history to know it repeats itself. God has not changed, so we may be certain that our need to obey Him has not changed. If we do not want to lose those things we hold dear, we, too, must be an obedient people. We must have hearts that are right with God and eager to follow Him.

MEMORY CHALLENGE

Copy Psalm 37:2 in this space.

Legacy

Read Ezra 2:1-2 and 70.

1. What key idea or phrase in Ezra 2:1 is found twice in Ezra 2:70?

2. Read Genesis 27:41-45. Why was Jacob afraid to return to his own land?

3. Read Genesis 31:1-3 and 32:3-12. What promise did Jacob have that it would be safe to return home?

4. What would be some of the reasons Jacob might not want to return home?

5. Many Israelites chose to stay in the land of their captivity, Babylon, instead of returning home to their legacy. Why might one have chosen to stay?

6. Why do you think those listed in Ezra 2 decided to return home?

A legacy, according to the dictionary, is a "bequest" or "a gift of money or property." The legacy of the children of Israel was that they were a chosen people who were given a chosen land in which they were to be set apart from the world in their obedience to and worship of Yahweh.

As covered earlier in the lessons, this promise was given to Abraham and carried through his son, Isaac, and then his son, Jacob, who became known as "Israel" (Genesis 32:28). Yet here the Israelites were captive in Babylon, and only a few chose to return to their own towns.

This was going to be a dangerous trip that would take four months. Going back would require sacrifice, for the land was unsettled, undeveloped, and full of enemies. The group returning was small and probably felt unprotected. So while 50,000 returned, most biblical scholars believe even more remained behind. In fact, the book of Ezra was written 50-55 years later, and the Jewish population in Babylon had exploded by that time.

Who would return under such hardship? Maybe a few carpetbaggers or those who preyed on hard times for their own gain. It is possible some thought they could prosper more in an undeveloped land. But probably most returned because they were called or felt committed. *So that you may know that I am the LORD, the God of Israel, who summons you by name* (Isaiah 45:3). Those who went back home made a choice to follow their legacy because the Lord called them home. They were committed to the task of restoring the Promised Land even if they weren't the most talented or athletic or intelligent. Jeannie McCullough, founder and teacher of Wisdom of the Word Bible Study, has worked with many volunteers. She has said many times that she would rather work with a faithful one-talent person than work with a ten-talent person who is undependable. God does not care about the importance of the job or our ability to do it, only our faithfulness to do it.

Our commitment to return home to God's Promised Land involves fear, such as Jacob and these 50,000 exiles experienced. It involves challenges, for no task for God is free of challenges. Yet it also contains promise—promise of a legacy that God had planned for Jacob and his family, for the Israelites, and for us. If we choose to return "home" by making our life with God, we, too, have a promise to achieve our legacy in Him. *"For I know the plans I have for you," declares the LORD, "plans to prosper you and not to harm you, plans to give you hope and a future"* (Jeremiah 29:11).

MEMORY CHALLENGE

Review Psalm 37:1 to answer who "they" refers to in verse 2.

The List

Read Ezra 5:6-10.

1. For this question only, use a concordance to find other places in God's Word where genealogies are listed.

2. Did you find Jesus Christ in any of these genealogies?

3. What is the purpose of genealogies in the Bible?

4. What do the following scriptures say regarding genealogies or a chosen line?

   1 Timothy 1:3-4

   Titus 3:9

   Ephesians 2:11-13

5. In the above scriptures, is God mandating that we are not to discover the roots of our ancestors, or is there a different point? (Remember, this is our personal interpretation of the scriptures, and we may not all agree.)

When it comes to genealogies in the Bible, the natural tendency is to skip them. After all, what's the point of the list? And who are those people anyway? Their names are hard to pronounce, and they seem to have little relevance to us.

Genealogies were important to the Jews. If one could not prove he was descended from Abraham, he was not considered a true Jew and was excluded from full participation in the community.

Throughout the Old Testament, all the genealogies were pointing to one Person. Abraham was promised he would be *a father of many nations* and *kings will come from you* (Genesis 17:5-6). But God also promised, *I will establish my covenant as an everlasting convenant between me and you and your descendants after you for the generations to come* (Genesis 17:7). So Abraham's line was royal, and the great kings of Israel, such as David and Solomon, came from him. Yet the everlasting promise was about eternal life established through Christ. Galatians 3:16 says, *The promises were spoken to Abraham and to his seed.* When we get to the genealogy of Jesus, scripture states, *A record of the genealogy of Jesus Christ the son of David, the son of Abraham: Abraham was the father of Isaac* (Matthew 1:1-2). From there the entire list leads to Christ.

This is important information for history and for us—to see how God always fulfills His promises. But when Christ died on the Cross, the list lost its meaning. For it no longer matters who we are or where we come from; salvation is offered to all people, and it comes through one Person, Jesus Christ. While genealogies may be interesting, they also are unimportant now that we have a Savior.

MEMORY CHALLENGE

Fill in the blanks:

"For like the _____ they will _____ _____, like _____ _____ they will soon _____ _____."

Psalm 37:_____

Lineage Lost

Read Ezra 2:59-63.

1. What was the question David asked in 1 Samuel 30:13?

2. How is this similar to the question asked of the descendants of Delaiah, Tobiah, Nekoda, Hobaiah, Hakkoz, and Barzillai?

3. In remembering the importance of genealogy in Israel, where did these families belong? (Or did they belong?)

4. To whom do you belong? Is this something of which you are certain, or does it seem to be a confusing issue?

5. Summarize the following scriptures according to how they relate to belonging.

Mark 9:41

John 14:1-3

John 15:19-20

Steven Kelley grew up in a dysfunctional family in Alabama. The father was out of the home, and an older brother had been removed from the home and subsequently adopted out. Steven was close to his younger sister, Sally, and she became his family. As a young man, his greatest talent was that he could run untouched down a football field.

But Steven longed to know his big brother. Having both a brother and a sister would make him feel more like he really belonged to a family. Though he had a full football scholarship to the University of Tennessee, he decided to move to his sister's college, Troy State. There something unbelievable happened.

He started running in the backfield with a player named Joe Jackson. As they talked and got to know each other, Steven was struck by some similarities. Teammates began to call them "doubles." Steven began to wonder if this could possibly be his brother. When he questioned his sister about it, she said, "Ask him if he was born on March 18, 1974." The answer proved that Joe was indeed Steve's biological brother. Now he had a family to whom he could belong.

Maybe family records could not be found for this group of people in the second chapter of Ezra, but with God there are no coincidences. Just as somehow Steven was drawn to this small school in Alabama to be close to his sister and play football and, therefore, found his brother, everyone has a place of belonging in God's kingdom.

According to Psalm 37:1-2, what will happen to evil men?

Livelihood and Location

Read Ezra 2:3-67.

1. From which locations listed did some of the exiles come? (Hint: Look at verses 21-35 and 59!)

2. Match the job description of these Levites with the job title:

   A. Assistants to Levites; dedicated by Solomon to Temple service — Gatekeepers

   B. Appointed by David to lift up voices of joyful music with accompanying instruments — Temple servants

   C. Authorized representatives of God; responsible to officiate at the altar in sacrificial rituals for the community of believers — Priests

   D. Guards of the Temple entrance — Singers

The lists in the second chapter of Ezra include the classification of exiles by families and clans (verses 3-20) and classification by location of residence (verses 21-35). The reason for these two listings is that there were two ways that being a Hebrew could be proven. The first was genealogy, and the second was by being a former resident or property owner in a particular city of Judah.

First Chronicles 24:7 lists the priests. One had to be a descendant of Aaron, God's original priest, to be a priest (Numbers 3:10). Numbers 16:40 warns against priests who could not prove their genealogy, so the group unable to find its records (verses 61-62) was excluded from service. Neither could the rejected priests eat the holy offerings until their status was decided (Numbers 18:9-10).

The status could only be determined through the use of the Urim and Thummim, two gems that were white on one side and black on the other. They fit in the breastplate of the holy priest's garment and were used to determine the will of God (Exodus 28:30-31 and Leviticus 8:8). When a question needed God's guidance, the high priest would pull out the stones and cast them as dice. If both sides showed white, there was affirmation from God. If both sides showed black, this was against the will of God. When God did not choose to answer, one stone was white while the other was black. An example of their probable use is in 1 Samuel 30:7-8, when David asked the high priest to bring the ephod to ask God if he, David, and his men should pursue a raiding party.

At this point in Israel's history it was believed that the Urim and Thummim had been lost during the destruction of Jerusalem and the Temple. With the destruction was the departure of the Shekinah glory as told in Ezekiel, chapters 8—11. Unless the Urim and Thummim could now be discovered, those desiring to be priests but having no records had no way to determine God's will in the matter.

Those in exile who had priestly records had great prospects in going back to Jerusalem because the rebuilding of the Temple would mean reestablishment of their livelihood. It would be similar to the idea of our country today being overrun and ruled by another nation that had different laws. This would put all lawyers out of business. But if the old government came back with the same laws, their livelihood would be restored. Therefore, about 1,000 priests were in the returning group.

But the Levites were a very small group, maybe only 75. Possibly because they performed less honorable functions in the Temple services, their group was not as anxious to return. When our churches have reunions, we tend to honor the pastors of the past, but not so much the janitors. It would be a similar comparison. The Levites had three classes: the regulars, the singers, and the doorkeepers.

The point of the list is to let us know that these people were truly Israelites who had a role to play in the rebuilding of their new nation. While studying the details may not be as interesting as studying the inspiration, it is often helpful in understanding God's Word so the inspiration can be based on truth.

Try to recite Psalm 37:2 correctly. Check for accuracy; repeat if necessary.

Love Offering

Read Ezra 2:68-69.

1. What do the following scriptures tell us about God's generosity?

   Psalm 84:11-12

   Psalm 86:5 and 15

   Psalm 107:9

   Psalm 111:3

   Ephesians 3:20

2. Look up Romans 5:5 in two different translations and write what it means to you. Then read below how it is translated in *The Message.*

   We're never left feeling shortchanged. Quite the contrary—we can't round up enough containers to hold everything God generously pours into our lives through the Holy Spirit (TM).

3. Give a personal example or two of how you have experienced God's generosity in your life.

God abounds in love to sinners. His enormous care shows in the beauty of the earth. His grace is sufficient in times of difficulty. In little ways He takes care of His own. His presence abides. Are we equally aware of His generosity?

God is not the government that gives welfare recipients just enough to scrape by; God is the Omnipotent One whose love is so expansive that He gave up the only Son He had to die in our place. The enormity of that one act reminds us that God is never thrifty, but pours out His Spirit upon us in incredible generosity.

Don't we want Christmas morning at our homes to be magnificently special? We want to give lavishly, and we hope everyone will love their gifts. We long to plan a marvelous day that provides wonderful memories for the entire family. We wish to prepare and serve the best food we have tasted all year. We want to be generous in our time, attention, love, and excitement on this day.

That is how God loves. Not just on Christmas morning, but every day of the year. He doesn't scrimp. He gives lavishly.

At a Christian university meeting of mentors of new students, the faculty and staff were instructed concerning their duties. Also, a $100 check was given to each mentor to offset expenses. During the course of the evening, the group was told of an incident involving a new student. The freshman had arrived in town the evening before he was able to move into the dorm, so he and his parents secured a motel room. The next morning they discovered that his car, with all of his belongings, had been stolen. To show care and support, the university took up a love offering. One mentor left feeling pleased about the $3 she had cheerfully given, but was chagrined when she witnessed another mentor placing her entire check in the offering. That mentor truly gave with the generosity of God.

Do we tend to think *little*? "How little can I give without guilt?" God thinks **BIG**—"how much do you need?"

MEMORY CHALLENGE

Find one other reference to evil men in the Bible.

Ezra

LESSON 3

■ A study of Ezra 3

DAY ONE

Altar

Read Ezra 3:1-2.

1. What happened in the seventh month?

2. What did the people who had assembled in Jerusalem begin to do?

3. How did they know how to build the altar?

4. The instructions for building the altar as well as the significance of this to God's people was given to Moses. Explain both of these ideas in the following scriptures.

   Exodus 20:24-26

   Deuteronomy 27:5-7

This altar constructed by Jeshua and Zerubbabel took about a day and was built as instructed in the earliest law of Moses. Stones from the field that could be found and carried were built one on top of another to make an altar. It was nothing fancy, but it represented the fundamentals in life for these people. It meant that they had put first things first and reestablished worship. This was even more important than building the Temple, for it meant all the regular sacrifices could now be offered at the appointed times. The feasts would be reestablished and all the offerings presented to God.

This altar was the altar of burnt offerings or sin offerings. It symbolized God's presence and protection and their nation's purpose to serve God alone. Sacrifices on the altar were necessary because they represented the people's seeking of God's direction, daily confession of their sins and commitment to living according to God's law. In modern-day terms, this altar represented the basics of life.

J. Vernon McGee in his commentary on Ezra reminisces about churches in the 1920s when money was short. Congregations would buy a lot, build a basement, and cover it with tar paper as a roof. Often the next step, building the main church, was never taken because the stock market crashed and the Depression

MEMORY CHALLENGE

Psalm 37:5

Trust in the LORD and do good; dwell in the land and enjoy safe pasture.

(NIV)

set in. So God's people worshiped in the basement. Now, that's really basic! But it did not keep the people from confessing their sins or praising the Lord. They had all they needed to worship.

This was true when God's children, under the direction of Zerubbabel and Jeshua, built the altar. It reminded them to confess their sins and praise the Lord. What a wonderful reminder for us too! In a day and age when life is very complicated, remembering that the basics are really all we need helps us to keep focused on God.

5. What do you believe are the basics by which we need to live?

6. The Bible records several episodes of people learning basic lessons of life through their experiences at the altar. Look up the following scriptures. Summarize the story and then pick the basic principle of life you feel this story represents.

    Genesis 22:8-18

    Judges 6:25-27

2 Samuel 24:18-25

1 Kings 18:16-39

MEMORY CHALLENGE

Begin the week by writing out Psalm 37:3 once or twice.

Anxiety

Read Ezra 3:3.

1. Which emotion did the exiles experience as they were building the altar?

2. How are fear and anxiety alike or different?

3. Read Genesis 3:8-12 to find the record of the first episode of fear in the world. Why did Adam tell God he was hiding?

4. Was it the fear of God or the fear of their enemies that caused the exiles to build the altar?

5. What role does God play in our lives when we are afraid? Read and record the following verses.

   Psalm 27:1

   Psalm 34:7-9

   Psalm 91:1-2

6. What does "fear of the Lord" mean?

   Proverbs 1:7

Proverbs 8:13

Job 28:28

Psalm 34:11-14

Fear comes in many forms. Some fears are caused by the intimidation of adversaries. For example, if little Johnny is being beaten up every day on the way to school by big bully Burt, he is wise to be afraid. Hopefully his anxiety will cause him to take some type of action, such as walking another route or asking an adult for help. This is normal, healthy fear because the situation truly carries some danger.

When fears begin to control us to the extent that we are afraid to go out of our houses, speak to strangers, or take a new job, then we have lost a healthy balance and are being ruled by our anxieties. God desires that we trust in Him to take care of us, knowing that this does not mean that our circumstances will be perfect, but that in all situations He will give us the strength to face them. It may be a difficult process, but we can once again learn to give our fears to God and have faith that He is powerful enough to take care of us. He who rules the universe can also control our anxieties.

The fear we need to consider in this lesson is fear caused by the reverence of God. Not only should we fear God's power and righteous consequences, but we should fear displeasing Him. If we live our lives in fear of displeasing God, we will have no need to try to hide from Him. We will be comfortable with Him if we have pleased Him.

MEMORY CHALLENGE

According to Psalm 37:3, in whom are we to put our trust?

Abundance

Read Ezra 3:4-6.

1. What did the people celebrate and why?

2. Read Leviticus 23:33-36. In addition to the offerings, what was the requirement for the first and eighth days?

3. Does this relate to us today? Why or why not?

4. In addition to the regular offerings and all appointed sacrifices, what else did they bring to the Lord? (See Ezra 3:5.)

5. Read Ephesians 1:6-7. What word or phrases describe how God gives His blessings to us?

6. When Jesus sent out the disciples, what did He say to them in Matthew 10:8?

7. Read Psalm 50:23 and Psalm 51:16-17. What kind of offering does God want from us?

God's people had been in captivity for 70 years before returning to their land. In spite of their fears, the people were anxious to follow all that the law of Moses required them to do in their worship of God. Even though today we do not observe and celebrate all the feasts, nor bring burnt offerings to the Lord, there are elements of the worship of these people that we can incorporate into our own worship.

These people knew God gave them all good things, and they freely gave back to Him. Can you say the same of your possessions, your life, your time? What happens when we give freely above and beyond what we may think is required of us? Have you ever had the joy of witnessing what God can do when we give with a "free will"?

Exodus 36:3-7 illustrates what God can do when we give according to the prompting of our hearts. *They received from Moses all the offerings the Israelites had brought to carry out the work of constructing the sanctuary. And the people continued to bring freewill offerings morning after morning. So all the skilled craftsmen who were doing all the work on the sanctuary left their work and said to Moses, "The people are bringing more than enough for doing the work the Lord commanded to be done." Then Moses gave an order and they sent this word throughout the camp: "No man or woman is to make anything else as an offering for the sanctuary." And so the people were restrained from bringing more, because what they already had was more than enough to do all the work.*

When God puts it in the hearts of His people to bring offerings and they do so freely, abundance is provided.

MEMORY CHALLENGE

Where are we to dwell and what are we to enjoy according to Psalm 37:3?

Almighty

Read Ezra 3:7-10.

1. Who sold building supplies to the exiles, and what were they paid in return for their supplies?

2. When the exiles began to build, how much time had passed since their arrival in Jerusalem?

3. Who was in charge of the workers?

4. At what point in the building process did the people stop to celebrate?

5. The foundation determines the stability of any wall, house, building, or life. Who has the Almighty provided as the foundation in our lives? (See Acts 4:11 and 1 Peter 2:4-6.)

6. Read 1 Peter 2:7-8. Why do some people stumble on this foundation?

God reminds us in Psalm 127:1, *Unless the LORD builds the house, its builders labor in vain. Unless the LORD watches over the city, the watchmen stand guard in vain.*

In Matthew 7:24-27, Jesus tells this story to His disciples: *Therefore everyone who hears these words of mine and puts them into practice is like a wise man who built his house on the rock. The rain came down, the streams rose, and the winds blew and beat against that house; yet it did not fall, because it had its foundation on the rock. But everyone who hears these words of mine and does not put them into practice is like a foolish man who built his house on sand. The rain came down, the streams rose, and the winds blew and beat against that house, and it fell with a great crash.*

While the exiles were building a physical foundation, Jesus' story in Matthew tells of our spiritual foundation. It is built on Christ himself as we obey Him, trust Him, pray to Him, study His Word, test His promises, and listen for His voice. He becomes our Foundation. As this occurs in our lives, we become stronger by relying on a Foundation that cannot be torn down.

As our Foundation, Jesus Christ strengthens our lives. He is immovable, unchanging, rock solid. Our lives are stable because we have a reliable Foundation. We should celebrate! God is good. He is to be praised. He is to be lifted up and glorified and given the credit He is due.

MEMORY CHALLENGE

What is your best technique to memorize scripture? Use it today and share it with your small group.

Acclamation

Read Ezra 3:10-11.

1. In a dictionary, look up the word "acclaim" and write the definition below.

2. Look up 1 Chronicles 16:8-10 and list the verbs from this passage.

3. Would you say acclamation is a spectator or participatory event?

4. Praise and acclamation lift up God's character or who He is. Write how each of the following scriptures describe God.

   Psalm 48:1

   Psalm 71:15

   Psalm 89:1-2

   Psalm 93:1

5. What part was assigned to music in praise in the Old Testament? Find 1 Chronicles 16:4-6 for the answer.

6. How are we to praise?

   Psalm 66:1-2

   Psalm 81:1-2

   Psalm 92:1-2

7. Think of a time that music has personally helped you to praise and, if comfortable, be ready to share this with your group.

Building the foundation of the Temple was a difficult job to accomplish. But when the hard work was done, no one looked for his own praise, but gave credit to God from whom all accomplishments come. The focus was God's goodness and His loving-kindness. The words from Psalm 136 were repeated over and over, *Give thanks to the LORD, for he is good. His love endures forever.* Much like our present-day responsive reading, a priest soloist would sing or chant the words and a choir would respond by repeating the words. The people were enthusiastic at this dedication service, and their acclamation was sincere.

J. Carl Laney, in his book *Ezra and Nehemiah,* tells us this passage teaches us three things. First, praise is a participatory happening. We are not truly praising God if we merely watch as others do it. Second, acclamation is a public expression of God's personhood and works. We are to lift up who He is and what He has done. Third, music enhances praise. In fact, it is hard to praise without music. The joy of a moment of acclamation is hard to capture without bursting into song. What valuable thoughts to help us learn to praise and acclaim our almighty God!

Look for an opportunity to apply some part of Psalm 37:3 to your day.

Ambivalence? Not!

Read Ezra 3:11-13.

1. Describe in your own words the celebration that took place upon the completion of the foundation.

2. How did the old men respond differently than the young men. List reasons why they reacted differently.

3. Have you ever been in a situation where joy and sorrow were intermingled? Explain.

What a fascinating scene! The foundation of the Temple had been laid, and the people were celebrating. There was excitement, joy, thanksgiving, praise, disappointment, and sorrow all mingled together. The emotions were overflowing, but they were mixed. Some of God's people were more happy than sad, but some of them were more sad than happy. Ambivalence was the one feeling that was not present. Emotions were intense one way or the other.

When our foundation is built in Christ, we thank Him for all the blessings He brings into our lives, and we praise Him simply for who He is. This can bring great joy to us as we are aware of God and bask in His presence. But sometimes His presence brings sorrow when we look at the world around us and see that it is not what God intended it to be. When God's ways are not honored, His people experience sadness over sin and how some people mistreat each other. When we compare the glory of God to the sinfulness of the world we live in, we are likely to experience mixed emotions.

Counselors have people in their offices every day who tell their stories of physical, emotional, or sexual childhood abuse. Knowing that this is not the way life was intended to be, many of them struggle as they deal with the sadness of this world. Those who feel the pain most intensely are those who have a concept of how good family life *could* be. They grieve over the loss of life as it should have been.

That was the scene when the Temple foundation was completed. For those who had never seen the original Temple in all its glory, this was great. They were excited and filled with joy. The older ones who had seen the former glory of the Temple felt some happiness at restoring what they had lost. But they realized the glory days were over and that this Temple would never compare to the beauty of Solomon's Temple, which was built with great wealth and enormous manpower. This was like replacing the Taj Mahal with a log cabin. That brought sorrow. The sorrow was due to the loss of the glory.

Sometimes the glory cannot be restored. Sometimes the consequences of our sins change life for us and there is sorrow over what is lost. Yet God always promises He will give our joy back if we keep ourselves centered in Him. Philippians 1:6 says, *He who began a good work in you will carry it on to completion until the day of Christ Jesus.* Jeremiah 29:11 reminds us, *"For I know the plans I have for you," declares the LORD, "plans to prosper you and not to harm you, plans to give you hope and a future."*

MEMORY CHALLENGE

Fill in the blanks:

"_____ in the LORD, _____ ____ _____;
dwell _____ _____ _____ and
_____ safe _____."

Psalm _____:_____

Ezra

■ A study of Ezra 4

DAY ONE

Suspects

Read Ezra 4, concentrating on verses 1-2.

1. What are the people who desired to help the tribes of Judah and Benjamin build the Temple called?

2. According to the following verses, who are the enemies of God?

   Matthew 13:37-39

   John 3:19 (keep in mind "light" refers to Christ)

   Colossians 1:21

3. What might have happened if the exiles had allowed these enemies of God to help?

4. If the enemies had been allowed to help, would that have constituted a partnership with unbelievers?

5. What does God's Word say about such compromising partnerships?

   1 Corinthians 5:12-13

   2 Corinthians 6:14

   1 Thessalonians 5:22

MEMORY CHALLENGE

Psalm 37:4

Delight yourself in the LORD and he will give you the desires of your heart.

(NIV)

6. What are some of the ways that we are drawn into compromising partnerships?

Who were these enemies of the tribes of Judah and Benjamin? After reading verse 2, we might assume that they were transplants brought here by Esarhaddon, king of Assyria. A little history lesson is needed to understand this.

After the death of Solomon in about 931 B.C., his son, Rehoboam, became the ruling king. He was unwise in his early decisions and quickly lost the support of ten of the tribes of Israel (see 1 Kings 12). Rehoboam was left to rule the tribes of Judah and Benjamin, which became known as the Southern Kingdom. Jeroboam became king of the remaining ten tribes, which became the Northern Kingdom. In 721 B.C. the ten tribes of the Northern Kingdom were carried into captivity by King Sargon of Assyria. Nebuchadnezzar destroyed Jerusalem in 586 B.C., taking most of the Southern Kingdom with him in Babylon.

These people now living in the Promised Land, called "enemies" in Ezra 4:1, were part of the Northern tribes carried into captivity by King Sargon. They had slowly migrated back to Israel and intermarried with the Samaritans. They did indeed worship Yahweh, but He was only one of their many gods.

Nevertheless, each national group made its own gods in the several towns where they settled, and set them up in the shrines the people of Samaria had made at the high places. The men from Babylon made Succoth Benoth, the men from Cuthah made Nergal, and the men from Hamath made Ashima; the Avvites made Nibhaz and Tartak, and the Sepharvites burned their children in the fire as sacrifices to Adrammelech and Anammelech, the gods of Sepharvaim. They worshiped the LORD, *but they also appointed all sorts of their own people to officiate for them as priests in the shrines at the high places. They worshiped the* LORD, *but they also served their own gods in accordance with the customs of the nations from which they had been brought* (2 Kings 17:29-33). This is why these people were enemies. They broke the first commandment, found in Exodus 20:3, *You shall have no other gods before* [or besides] *me.*

What were these people really suggesting? What were their motives? Beware of taking others at face value, for Satan parades as an angel of light (2 Corinthians 11:14). Ask God to help you to be discerning.

If we are people-pleasers, we might be especially tempted to form compromising partnerships. We do not want to cause any waves or "to rock the boat," so we give up in the name of peace, often to discover it is only a temporary peace. If evil creeps in, there will also be chaos.

What happens in compromising partnerships? First of all, the good is joined with evil. Unless the evil is confronted and chooses to change, the good will fight a continual battle for righteousness. Evil often is subtle in these situations and creeps in; the good becomes diluted and lowers its standards. If the situation progresses, the evil can become stronger than the good. Second Corinthians 6:14-15 in *The Message* tells us, *Don't become partners with those who reject God. How can you make a partnership out of right and wrong? That's not partnership; that's war. Is light best friends with dark? Does Christ go strolling with the Devil? Do trust and mistrust hold hands?*

A.W. Tozer, in his book *God Tells the Man Who Cares*, states, "In a fallen world like ours unity is no treasure to be purchased at the price of compromise. Loyalty to God, faithfulness to truth and the preservation of a good conscience are jewels more precious than gold." The exiles recognized this and would not make a compromising partnership.

MEMORY CHALLENGE

Read Psalm 37:4 aloud several times and write it down as you begin to memorize it this week.

Selective

Read Ezra 4:3.

1. What was the answer Zerubbabel and company gave the enemies of Judah and Benjamin?

2. If we are going to work for God, what does He require of us? Look up the following scriptures to find some answers.

    Deuteronomy 10:12

    1 Samuel 15:22

    Micah 6:8

    John 14:15

3. The Bible teaches us that there is a progression of evil when we choose to disobey. Summarize the important points of these scriptures in Proverbs as they relate to the progression of evil.

    Proverbs 1:10-11, 15-16

    Proverbs 2:12-15

Proverbs 4:18-19

4. Explain how a similar situation (where God's people had to say "you have no part") recurred later. (See Nehemiah 2:20.)

5. Would you say God's people, the exiles, were bold in turning the enemy away? Why or why not?

6. From memory or by using a concordance for this question only, pick a favorite scripture or two about being bold for the Lord that you can share with your group.

Matthew 22:14 (RSV) states, *For many are called, but few are chosen.* Have you ever wondered what this means? This verse is the conclusion to the parable of the wedding banquet. The king had prepared a wedding banquet for his son and sent his servants out to bring back the guests. But those who were invited were indifferent toward the invitation and chose instead to go about their own business. So the king said those invited did not deserve to come, and he sent the servants into the streets to gather whoever would come. The group was assembled when the king walked in and spotted one man without wedding attire. He asked him how it was that he got into the banquet without proper attire. The man was speechless, and the king had the servants throw him out. Then the king proclaimed that many are invited, but few are chosen.

This parable seems to indicate that all of us have an opportunity to choose God's kingdom, but we make our own decision. We can be too busy to be available when God calls us, or we may come but not be "properly dressed" for the occasion. Coming when called and being "properly dressed" when we arrive has to do with the condition of our hearts.

In Ezra 4, obedience and avoiding partnerships with evil both seem to be prerequisites to being ready for God's invitation. God is selective—if we do not choose to follow Him, He will not choose us.

Matthew 25:31-46 records the judgment of the nations. *When the Son of Man comes in his glory, and all the angels with him, he will sit on his throne in heavenly glory. All the nations will be gathered before him, and he will separate the people one from another as a shepherd separates the sheep from the goats. He will put the sheep on his right and the goats on his left* (verses 31-33).

Then the King will say to those on his right, "Come, you who are blessed by my father; take your inheritance" (verses 31-34). *Then he will say to those on his left, "Depart from me, you who are cursed, into the eternal fire prepared for the devil and his angels"* (verse 41). Obviously, we will not automatically be included in God's kingdom. We must follow God and if we do not, we can have no part.

When we're doing God's work, we think we have to let everyone help. What does this passage teach us about that? Maybe having a heart right with God is very important for ministry. We must be selective in who is part of the ministry team if we want to avoid compromising partnerships.

Does this mean we have to be perfect? Not one of us is. We are perfect only as covered by the blood of Christ, which is God's grace. This also does not mean that we minister as a clique. Ministry has little to do with friendships, in the beginning at least. It has to do with partnerships in God's work because we are brothers and sisters in Christ. We don't exclude people because we don't like their personality; we exclude them only if their hearts are evil and they choose not to change.

It is not an easy task to be selective. It takes discernment and boldness. But we must always keep in mind the diluted state of our ministry if we are not selective. As in everything, God will guide us and give us wisdom.

MEMORY CHALLENGE

In whom are we to delight ourselves?

Sour Grapes

Read Ezra 4:4-5.

1. What did the people of the land around the exiles set out to do?

2. Fear can sometimes bring about discouragement. Read and summarize the following verses.

    Deuteronomy 1:21

    1 Kings 19:2-5

3. What are some other causes of discouragement? Find the answers in the following scriptures.

    Numbers 32:6-7

    2 Corinthians 4:8-9

    Colossians 3:21

4. In the following scriptures, find some remedies against discouragement.

    Psalm 55:22

Mark 6:31

Luke 21:27-28

2 Corinthians 4:16-18

5. How do you personally handle discouragement? Do you rise to the challenge, ignore it, get depressed by it, or something totally different? Share your answer with your group if you are comfortable.

Discouragement is certainly a part of the world in which we live. While God protects us in our circumstances, He does not always protect us from our circumstances. Therefore, we can expect to deal with discouragement on a regular basis in a fallen world. Learning how to handle it is a key to avoiding spiritual defeat.

Isn't it interesting that as soon as the exiles told the unbelievers that they could have no part in the building of God's Temple, the outsiders turned against them? That was truly sour grapes! Refusal to give in to evil brings opposition. Will God's work ever go forth unchallenged? Probably not, so when the first plan of the unbelievers did not work they developed a new plan.

The unbelievers' plan was to harass the exiles first, then to threaten them, and finally to send false counselors. And, honestly, it worked. The building stopped for 15 years because the exiles were discouraged. Most biblical scholars believe they gave up too easily and let their discouragement overcome them. Eventually this led to distractions, and the people began building their own homes instead of the Temple (Haggai 1:1-15).

How do we handle discouragement today? Some of the above scriptures indicate that discouragement is a feeling brought on by other people or circumstances that are frightening. Maybe discouragement is really caused by a lack of courage to face a circumstance or person who is difficult. Handling a distressing situation certainly requires courage. Even if things don't turn out the way we would like, taking courage helps us avoid letting the situation control us through discouragement. Going to the Lord for our courage when we don't have it is certainly a good solution. Psalm 27:14 says, *Wait on the Lord: be of good courage, and he shall strengthen thine heart: wait, I say, on the Lord* (KJV). Psalm 42:11 encourages, *But O my soul, don't be discouraged. Don't be upset. Expect God to act!* (TLB).

MEMORY CHALLENGE

Fill in the blanks:

"Do not _____ because of _____ _____ or be _____ of those who do _____. For like the _____ they will _____ _____; like _____ _____ they will soon _____ _____. _____ in the Lord _____ _____ _____; dwell _____ _____ _____, and _____ safe _____. _____ yourself in the _____ and _____ _____ _____ you the _____ of your _____."

Psalm 37:1-4

Sabotage

Read Ezra 4:6-12.

1. Were Ahasuerus and Xerxes the same person? Check your Bible footnotes and also Esther 1:12 and Daniel 9:1.

2. Xerxes reigned from 486 to 464 B.C. and was followed by Artaxerxes from 464 to 424 B.C. Does this mean that verse 6 and verse 7 of Ezra 4 are talking about two separate events?

3. What did these men who wrote the letter call themselves in Ezra 4:11?

4. As we prepare to study the charges brought against the exiles in Day 5, think about how it feels to be falsely accused. Write a couple of ideas about that here.

5. David was feeling falsely accused in Psalm 7. Read the psalm and record some of the major points.

Steven Linscott was a student at Chicago's Emmaus Bible College in 1980 when a young nursing student was brutally murdered in Oak Park, a nearby suburb. Trying to help solve the crime, Steven told police investigators of a dream he had the night of the murder. Eventually police arrested Steven, taking this information as the confession of a psychotic killer. He was convicted on virtually no evidence, spent three and a half years in prison, and twelve years clearing his good name. In his book, *Maximum Security,* Steven tells what it is like to be falsely accused.

First of all, being falsely accused is a very humbling experience. To go from being a Bible college student involved in ministry and planning to be a missionary to being a prisoner accused of murder is more than a bit humbling. Second, being falsely accused is frightening. What if one can never prove his innocence? What kind of hardships must be endured? For Steven Linscott it meant three and a half years of wrongful imprisonment. Third, being falsely accused is time-consuming. Maybe one wants to spend the hours of the day in a different way, but time and energy must be spent in clearing one's name.

The Jewish exiles experienced many of these same feelings. They had no intentions at this point of becoming a powerful nation and overthrowing other governments. They simply were trying to restore the Promised Land and reestablish their worship. Their goal was simple, and it included hurting no one else. Yet if the enemies could not be included, they were not simply going to leave it as "sour grapes," but move on to sabotage. If they did not get their way, their plan was to ruin it for the others.

We must be careful as we work against others' plans. What are our reasons? Are they pure in the Lord as shown to us through His Word or wise counsel or meditation? Have we stopped to examine our reasons and make sure they are pleasing God? Taking time to check our own hearts keeps us from falsely accusing others. This is pleasing to God.

If we delight ourselves in the Lord, what will happen?

Search and Reply

Read Ezra 4:12-22.

1. What is the description of Jerusalem that these "servants" of the king give?

2. What do the servants claim as their motive for informing the king?

3. Is motive important with God? Read and summarize the following verses.

   1 Chronicles 28:9

   Jeremiah 12:3

   Matthew 5:8

   Hebrews 4:12

4. Do you have a situation in your life in which it is hard to have pure motives? Take some time now to meditate about this before the Lord, recording some of your thoughts below. Remember to pray for forgiveness if necessary and for purity of heart.

A little-known shortstop by the name of Jerry Terrell played baseball for the Kansas City Royals in their glory years of 1976-80. His strength was his defensive play, but he was only an average hitter. He was rarely a starting player; instead, he was usually used as a substitute for an injured or tired teammate, sometimes playing for long periods at a time. But Jerry was a team leader and a man whom all the players respected and admired. He was a Christian and made his faith in Christ public knowledge.

Near the end of the season one year, when it seemed as if the Royals had a shot at the World Series, the management made a decision to send Jerry to the Triple A farm club in Omaha, Nebraska. They needed his slot for a player who they thought could help them more through the playoffs. Fred White, one of the Royals' radio announcers, decided to interview Jerry about his *demotion*.

Most people are not interviewed about demotions. We let them go. But Fred White knew what kind of man Jerry Terrell was and that many people in Kansas City would be sad to see him go. This was an opportunity for a farewell address.

That interview was incredible. Jerry Terrell basically said, "I want to be with the Royals especially when there is that once in a lifetime chance to get a World Series ring. But more than that, I want to do what God's will is for my life. If God's plan is for me to play ball in Omaha, then that is what I want to do more than anything. There are souls in Omaha to win, too, and my life is committed to His plan."

Jerry modeled a profound lesson about motives. Why was he playing baseball? Was he playing for the money or his own glory? No. He was playing because it was God's will for his life, and where he was playing was irrelevant. His heart was pure, which kept his priorities right and his ability to deal with disappointment high. This demotion wasn't about ability; it was about trusting God with the circumstances of life. Jerry had the right motives.

What a challenge to have the right motives. What a difference it would have made for the exiles if the people around them had had pure motives. But they did not and instead used false accusations. Such difficulties will occur. May we have the strength and grace to face them as well as did a little-known baseball player by the name of Jerry Terrell.

MEMORY CHALLENGE

Taking Psalm 37:4 in context, along with your biblical knowledge, what do you believe this verse means?

Standstill

Read Ezra 4:23-24.

1. What happened as soon as King Artaxerxes' letter was read to Rehum and Shimshai and associates? What method did these associates use to stop the work.

2. Until when did God's work stay at a standstill?

3. When Nehemiah asked about the conditions in Jerusalem, what did he find out? Read Nehemiah 1:1-4.

4. Is it possible that when the exiles were compelled to stop, there was force used on them and the work already completed? What hints would you have of this from the Nehemiah passage?

5. The exiles were at a standstill in fulfilling what God had called them to do. What do you think happens in our lives during a time of standstill from God's plans?

6. What happened in the lives of the exiles during this standstill? Find the answer in what Haggai prophesied about this to the people in Haggai 1:1-15. Also, find in today's scriptures and the passage in Haggai how we know this is the same time period.

7. What was the result of Haggai's prophecy?

When circumstances bring us to a place of standing still, we are vulnerable. Most of us do better when we are moving, and being still is a challenge. But there is much standing still in life. We may be "on hold" waiting for the birth of a new baby, or waiting to graduate from college, or waiting for a husband or wife to become a believer, or even waiting to be released from prison. It's like the old song says, "Just biding my time."

In our Christian life we cannot stand still for long. But when we do, it's a time to *Be still, and know that I am God* (Psalm 46:10). It's a time to regroup, catch our breath and remember we're still in a battle for our souls. God will affirm in us at this time what we are to do, whether it's reaffirming the old direction or guiding us into a totally new one. Second Chronicles 20:17 says, *You will not have to fight this battle. Take up your positions; stand firm and see the deliverance the LORD will give you, O Judah and Jerusalem. Do not be afraid; do not be discouraged. Go out to face them tomorrow, and the LORD will be with you.* At a standstill, take the time to know how to move forward.

A standstill is temporary. Pretty soon we will be moving again, either forward or backward. Each day we have a choice to give the day to God or let Satan have it. Many people want to believe it's okay not to choose right now, thinking that when they are ready they will choose. Unfortunately, "no choice" is a choice for Satan. He never stands still in our lives. It is like a muscle that is not used; it does not remain strong and healthy, but shrinks and weakens. If the work of God in your life comes to a standstill, before long it will start to move backward. The purpose of standing still is to reevaluate, not to remain stuck.

What will the exiles do with their standing still? What will we do with our standing still? Take some time to ask God where you are in life—standing still, moving forward, or moving backward. Let Him affirm in you your place, and help you make a correction.

MEMORY CHALLENGE

Write Psalm 37:4 from memory. Check your answer for accuracy.

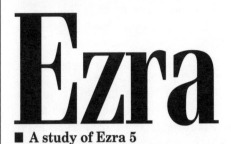
Ezra

■ A study of Ezra 5

DAY ONE

Developments

Read Ezra 5, concentrating on verses 1-2.

1. What occurred in Ezra 5:1?

2. How did the people respond to the prophecy (verse 2)?

3. Who helped the people begin to rebuild the Temple?

4. Another word for what Haggai and Zechariah did might be "exhortation." Look this word up in the dictionary or a Bible concordance and define it.

5. There seems to be a pattern here of (1) a word connection, (2) lay leadership responding, and (3) spiritual leadership working alongside the laity. Look up the following scriptures that also give an example of the people responding to prophecy. Record the basic facts.

   Jonah 3:1-10

   Haggai 1:5-13

   Mark 1:1-5

6. Look up the following scriptures that demonstrate leadership working alongside the laity as a model. Record the basic facts.

   Joshua 1:1-5

   Judges 4:4-10

   Matthew 14:15-21

7. Can you think of a personal example that you have been involved in or observed where a word of correction was spoken, laity responded, and the leadership then worked alongside the laity?

MEMORY CHALLENGE

Psalm 37:5

*Commit your way to the LORD;
trust in him and he will do this.*

(NIV)

What a powerful scene! The work on the house of God had come to a standstill and no one seemed to be concerned. In fact, as we discovered in the last lesson, the people had begun to build their own houses and plant their own vineyards. They had gone on with life by getting married, having babies, raising children, decorating their homes, and trying to enjoy themselves. They knew the crops and cattle had not done well but had not stopped to consider why. Then Haggai came along to deliver the Word of the Lord. He said, *"Give careful thought to your ways. . . . You expected much, but see, it turned out to be little. What you brought home, I blew away. Why?" declares the LORD Almighty. Because of my house, which remains a ruin, while each of you is busy with his own house"* (Haggai 1:7, 9).

And the beauty is that the people responded! Three weeks after Haggai prophesied, the people resumed work on the Temple! They took to heart the idea that they were faithless in building their own houses instead of the Lord's. They believed that was the reason they had been plagued with drought, which produced poor crops and cattle. The sudden developments in Jerusalem occurred because the people heard a word of correction—and corrected!

Who is this man, Haggai? He was believed to have been born in Babylon, later returning with the first set of exiles. His book of two chapters took place over a period of four months with four dated messages. The first message, basically stated above (Haggai 1:2-11), was spoken to Zerubbabel and Joshua, the son of the high priest. The second message delivered to the people (Haggai 1:13) stated, *"I am with you," declares the LORD.* Now look up Haggai 2 and find the last two dates for messages. Record the messages for each date below, the date itself and any response the people and their leaders had. (For clarity, use *The Living Bible* for this question if possible.)

Haggai could be described as a man with his feet on the ground, a man who was dependable. He wanted facts. Haggai spoke to the conscience of the people, and his messages went deep and were hurtful. This brought developments in the people's lives, for they listened and obeyed.

Ezra 5 also tells us of the prophet, Zechariah, a grandson of Iddo, whose own father had died before he assumed the priesthood. He was a man of vision and more of a dreamer than Haggai. Zechariah appealed to the emotions of the people, and spoke to their hearts. Two months after Haggai first prophesied, Zechariah began to prophesy. He spoke, as any prophet, as a representative of God. The book of Zechariah is full of his prophecies, but for a specific example related to Jerusalem, turn to chapter 8 and summarize the basic points below.

Not only is this a powerful scene, but it is a powerful example. The exiles had lost their focus. They came back to Jerusalem to return to the land promised them and to resume their worship, but they had gotten sidetracked. God laid His Word of correction on these two godly men, Haggai and Zechariah, who spoke the Word to the people. The people resumed their intended focus, and the work of rebuilding the Temple was restarted. Haggai and Zechariah did not stop there, but they entered into the work themselves.

Is there ever a time that the Lord lays a correction on our hearts in which we are not to be a part of the process? If we see a need to refocus within His Body, does He ever call us to speak the Word to others but not to participate in the work ourselves? Those who receive the vision have to join in making the vision happen. Leaders who do not want to join in the work are suspect. What a short sentence at the end of Ezra 5:2, but so powerful! *And the prophets of God were with them.*

MEMORY CHALLENGE

Write out Psalm 37:5 (on a separate sheet of paper) two or three times as preparation for memorizing it this week.

Detection

Read Ezra 5:3-5.

1. What does "detection," the title for this day, mean? If you need help, feel free to use a dictionary.

2. Why do you think Tattenai, Shethar-Bozenai, and associates asked for the names of those constructing the Temple?

3. Do people tend to look for the name of someone to blame? Summarize the following scriptures to help with this answer.

    Genesis 3:8-12

    Genesis 3:13

    Genesis 4:8-9

4. Second Corinthians 8:21 states, *For we are taking pains to do what is right, not only in the eyes of the LORD but also in the eyes of men.* When we do right in the eyes of the Lord, are we ever blamed by men anyway? If so, what is our protection? (See Ezra 5:5.)

5. Find the following scriptures that bring encouragement about God's eye being on His people. If you are comfortable doing so, highlight these passages in your Bible. Record only your favorite.

    Deuteronomy 11:11-12

    2 Chronicles 16:9

    Psalm 33:18

    1 Peter 3:12

In many ways Ezra 5 is a repeat of Ezra 4 with a different result. In chapter 4, the rebuilding was opposed, and the enemies succeeded in bringing the work to a standstill for 15 years. But in Ezra 5, when the prophets exhorted that the house of God must not remain in disrepair while they built their own homes, the people got right to work again. Round two starts with more opposition. But this time, not only was the eye of the Lord upon His people, but the people *trusted* in His eye of protection.

Catherine Marshall was the wife of the beloved chaplain of the Senate and pastor of New York Avenue Presbyterian Church in Washington, D.C., Peter Marshall. Peter died an untimely death at age 46, leaving Catherine an ill-prepared widow. She was only in her thirties and had hardly held a job, for she had married Peter when he was already a pastor and she had played the expected role of a pastor's wife. While a wonderful husband, Peter had not left her in good financial shape at the time of his death. Suddenly Catherine was the sole supporter of herself and her nine-year-old son, Peter John.

Thankfully, the elders of her church allowed Catherine and Peter Jr. to live in the parsonage while she decided what she was to do. They were all very helpful in giving her advice and leads for jobs, but something held her back. She had been an English major in college and had always wanted to write. She had felt the Lord's presence in her life even in the hospital room where she told her deceased husband's body good-bye. She knew the eyes of the Lord were upon her and that He had a plan for her. *I will instruct thee and teach thee in the way which thou shalt go: I will guide thee with mine eye* (Psalm 32:8, KJV).

Catherine, against all advice except God's, decided to write. It would not be a set income, but she decided to act upon the Lord's protection. So she started by compiling a set of Peter Marshall's sermons and titled it *Mr. Jones, Meet the Master.* The volume did very well, and the rest of Catherine Marshall's life is history. She gave us over 20 books with spiritual insight, including *A Man Called Peter, Beyond Ourselves, Something More, To Live Again,* and *Meeting God at Every Turn.* She even brought us a best-seller, *Christy.*

Sometimes, knowledge that the eye of the Lord is upon us is not enough. We must trust this knowledge and act upon it. Catherine Marshall's life is an example of this and because of it, God richly blessed her. The exiles, too, were protected and blessed each time they trusted that the eye of the Lord was upon them. Let's watch this as we continue to study Ezra.

MEMORY CHALLENGE

What does the memory verse for this week command us to do with our way?

Diligence

Read Ezra 5:6-10.

1. How did the officials of Trans-Euphrates describe the work that was being done in the district of Judah?

2. "Diligence" can be defined as "faithful application to one's work" (*Guideposts Family Concordance*). Summarize the following scriptures regarding diligence. (To actually find the word "diligence," you may have to use the King James translation of the Bible.)

   Zechariah 6:15

   Proverbs 4:23

   Hebrews 6:11

   2 Peter 3:14

3. What is the one area in which you presently feel God is calling you to be diligent?

4. What are the thoughts of your heart about your area of diligence? Does there need to be confession? Are you unsure how to proceed, and do you need God's guidance? Does there seem to be a roadblock that brings turmoil? Are you feeling confident in God that He is in charge of this area of your life and you are right on target? However you see fit, take some time now to outline some of your thoughts; pray and meditate upon what God is saying to you.

Just when the exiles had started again on the Temple, a new face appeared—Tattenai—who questioned what they were doing. Possibly, however, Tattenai was not acting as an enemy so much as he was being diligent in his work. The Persian Empire was in turmoil at this time and so he needed to be careful about anything happening in his jurisdiction, which included Judah as part of Syria and Palestine.

Cyrus died in 530 B.C., leaving his son, Cambyses, as king. There was rebellion, and Cambyses had to fight to secure his throne. One of his contenders was his brother, Smerdis, whom he had killed. However, this did not end the trouble for Gaumata, an Egyptian nobleman who was able to pull off a deception in which he claimed to be Smerdis. This caused confusion as to whether Smerdis was dead or alive. Much of the empire followed this pretender until Cambyses, in 522 B.C., took his own life. At that time the army backed Cyrus's distant cousin, Darius, as the rightful successor to the throne. Darius and the army were able to overthrow the pretender. However, to secure the throne, he faced two more years of putting down rebellions.

It was during Darius's second year that the Temple work was restarted. As a conscientious governor, Tattenai wanted to know who was doing this work and who had authorized it. Possibly these men were enemies of the new king and did not have his permission to work on this structure. Maybe Tattenai was simply diligently doing his job.

But, praise God, the exiles were also diligently doing the job for which they had returned to Jerusalem. They had already discovered that just returning home was not enough. It did not end the problems with smooth sailing the rest of the way. Instead, they had to remain diligent. They had to continue "faithful application to one's work" if it was to be completed. Some lessons, no matter how old, never change.

MEMORY CHALLENGE

Fill in the blanks:

"_____ your _____ to the _____;

_____ in _____ and he _____

_____ _____."

Psalm _____ :5

Destroyed

Read Ezra 5:11-12.

1. Who is the great king referred to in verse 11? (See 1 Kings 6:1 for help if needed.)

2. What is the reason the exiles had to rebuild the Temple?

3. When the people were deported to Babylon, not only was the Temple destroyed, but so much more. Think of all the destruction of war and describe what else was lost to the Israelites. Consider more than just material things.

4. Not only were buildings destroyed, but lives were destroyed as well. Summarize the following scriptures regarding rebuilding lives.

   Jeremiah 30:17

   Joel 2:25-27

   Psalm 23:1-2

5. A building has to be built from the ground up. In Lesson 3, we studied how the foundation has to be laid first. Ezra 5 tells us how the work is being done with large stones and by placing timbers in the walls. When a life is destroyed, it must also be rebuilt from the ground up. What large "stone" needs to be laid in a foundation? Find at least two scriptures to back up some of your answers.

From the time Louise was a little girl she had collected teacups. When her family would go on vacation, she would buy a cup as her souvenir. As she grew older, others got into the act by giving her cups for special occasions. By the time she was 40, she had collected 35 teacups from different places and people for different occasions.

Louise had a special friend, Angela, who cleaned her house on a regular basis. One week a relative of Angela's came to help clean, but she accidentally knocked a cup rack off the wall and sent it crashing to the floor. Nine cups lay splintered in a thousand pieces, and Angela was deeply upset and embarrassed over the accident.

Occasionally, Louise would run home from work for lunch, and on this day decided to do so. She was surprised to find her friend's car gone when she drove up to the house, but figured Angela had gone to run an errand. Upon entering the house, she discovered her cups in pieces on the dining room table. Horrified, and knowing Angela was sick with hurt, she hurried to finish eating so she could leave and not face her friend. Louise was too upset, herself, to try to comfort Angela.

When work was over, Louise dreaded going home and facing the broken teacups, but more so, Angela's apologies. However, upon entering the house, she saw all nine teacups on the rack looking perfectly normal. Louise stared. How could this be? Had she dreamed the whole thing? The cups had been in pieces on the table! Louise walked closer and examined the teacups. There she saw cracks and chips, but more than that, hours of work restoring the teacups to as beautiful a product as possible. The steady hand and patience required amazed Louise! It was like a miracle.

How did Angela not give up in despair and forget the whole rebuilding project? She took two big pieces that fit and glued them and continued to work from there. She put one large stone (or piece) on stone and fitted timber in between. She laid a foundation and filled in.

We know our cornerstone is Jesus Christ and without Him there is no foundation in our lives (Ephesians 2:20). He reveals the Father who builds His kingdom on His Word, His name, and His Son. When our lives are destroyed in some way, going back to the foundation is always the answer. Getting right with the Son, believing in His name, and knowing His Word will allow us to rebuild our lives.

MEMORY CHALLENGE

How does Psalm 37:5 relate to this day's theme of rebuilding a destroyed life?

Decree

Read Ezra 5:13-16.

1. In defending their position, the exiles claimed that Cyrus issued a decree to rebuild the house of God. Is this true? If so, where is the biblical proof? (Hint: This can be found in Ezra.)

2. Does the exiles' statement that Cyrus sent the gold and silver articles from the temple in Babylon back to Jerusalem give any strength to their defense? How?

3. A decree may be defined as "a judicial decision" (Webster) or a law or edict. Summarize the following references where a decree was ordered.

   Esther 3:8-14

   Daniel 6:6-9

   Luke 2:1-3

4. Would you say the king or governor in the above scriptures used the decree for good or evil?

5. How does God use His decrees or laws?

   Exodus 18:20

   Deuteronomy 11:8 and 13-15

   Psalm 119:97-101

   John 15:10

The United States has always had a fairly complicated system of making and regulating laws. We elect legislative bodies on different levels of government who debate laws before they are ever passed, if indeed they are passed. Then we have mayors or governors or presidents who must sign the decrees before they become law. And if the correctness of the law is ever questioned against our local, state, and federal constitutions, then we have a body of judges who decide if the decree is legal. Our system, while having its own problems, is based on checks and balances.

In the Old Testament times, issuing a decree was a simple matter for the one in charge. He was the supreme ruler and could basically decree anything he so desired. For example, Haman was able to get Xerxes to put in writing an edict to attack and kill all the Jews in the king's province on the 13th day of the first month. Yet because of the intervention of God through Esther and Mordecai, Xerxes issued another decree that allowed the Jews to defend themselves on that day (Esther 8:8).

Darius was also fooled by jealous advisers who wanted the king to decree that no one could pray to any god but him. This is what placed Daniel, the adviser he depended upon the most, in the lions' den. But this decree also failed when God intervened by closing the mouths of the lions.

In the case of the exiles, the decree was on their side; it was their defense. Yet in a sense, that is irrelevant, for God will accomplish His purpose in spite of man. But the beauty of the decree is that even when man may use it for evil, God always uses it for good. This is a reflection of His character, for His intentions for man are good. God does not make a law to put us in a difficult position like Darius did to Daniel, or Xerxes did to Esther. God's laws are for our benefit.

The law of the LORD is perfect, reviving the soul. The statutes of the LORD are trustworthy, making wise the simple. The precepts of the LORD are right, giving joy to the heart. The commands of the LORD are radiant, giving light to the eyes. The fear of the LORD is pure, enduring forever. The ordinances of the LORD are sure and altogether righteous. They are more precious than gold, than much pure gold; they are sweeter than honey, than honey from the comb. By them is your servant warned; in keeping them there is great reward (Psalm 19:7-11).

MEMORY CHALLENGE

Psalm 37:5 admonishes us to trust God. What does this mean to you?

Decision

Read Ezra 5:17.

Verse 17 records the request of Tattenai and associates for a search to see if there was a decree. Then they requested a decision from Darius so they would know if they should let the exiles proceed with building the Temple. We, too, are going on a search for this day's assignment. The different decrees and dates you discover will hopefully lead to a decision regarding how all the historical information fits together. The purpose is to clarify the events thus far and prepare us for the coming events.

On the back of this page, you will find a time line that already lists a few dates. By looking back at the lessons in Ezra and checking biblical references, you will see the time line grow. Feel free to use the whole page, making some lines (perpendicular to the time line) long and others short to fit in all the words you want to use. If you stumble upon any dates not requested, feel free to add them to the time line. Begin now by looking up the answer to each question below and place the answer on the time line.

1. Go back to the Introduction to Ezra at the beginning of this study. The first paragraph at the top of the second column gives the date Babylon fell to Persia. Record the date on the time line.

2. Still in the Introduction, but on the second page, first paragraph, is the date of 450-430 B.C. Write in the significance of this date on your time line.

3. In Lesson 1 of Ezra, Day One, find the dates of Cyrus's reign in the second paragraph. Fill this in on the time line along with the significance of the date, 539 B.C.

4. Turn to Lesson 4 of Ezra, Day One, page 2. The paragraph that begins with the death of Solomon has several dates. Find and put on the time line the significance of 586 B.C.

5. Continue to Day Four of Lesson 4 and in question 2 find the dates Xerxes and Artaxerxes reigned.

6. Day Six of Lesson 4 has a date in the answer to question 7. Find this on the time line and fill in from this question what happened at that time.

7. Find the date on the time line that Cyrus began to reign in Babylon. Read Ezra 1:1 and place on the time line the year of the proclamation of Cyrus to return to Jerusalem. (Hint: Add one year, for the first year, to the Cyrus date on the time line.)

8. According to Ezra 3:1, what would be the year the Feast of Tabernacles was again celebrated in Jerusalem? (Hint: This was actually a year after Cyrus's proclamation.)

9. What happened in the second year after the arrival in Jerusalem, according to Ezra 3:8?

10. Four years after the Temple construction began, it came to a standstill. Put this date on the time line.

11. The second year of Darius's reign brought a new development. Find this event in Ezra 4:24.

12. Ezra 6:15 gives an important date and event. Record these on the time line.

13. What would have occurred in the year 516 B.C. according to Ezra 6:19?

14. Ezra 7:6, 8 tells of an event that occurred in 458 B.C. Record the event on the time line.

MEMORY CHALLENGE

Write Psalm 37:5 from memory in the space provided below.

B. C.

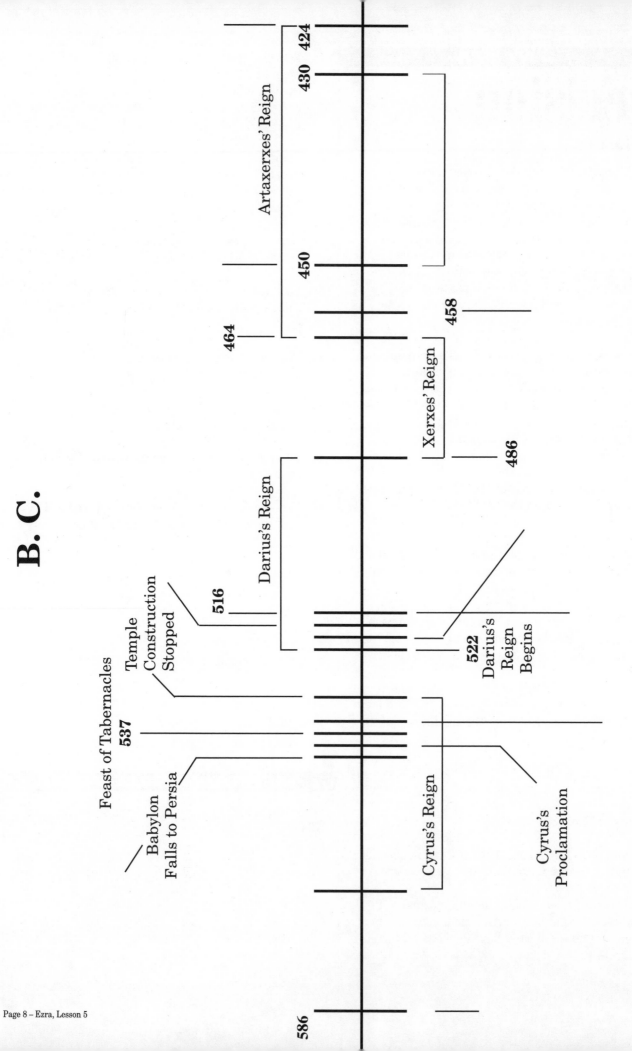

586

Feast of Tabernacles
537

Babylon
Falls to Persia

Temple
Construction
Stopped

516

Darius's Reign

Cyrus's Reign

Cyrus's
Proclamation

522
Darius's
Reign
Begins

Xerxes' Reign

486

458

464

450

Artaxerxes' Reign

430 **424**

Ezra

■ A study of Ezra 6

DAY ONE

Copy Found

Read Ezra 6:1-5.

1. What was the purpose of King Darius's order, and what was the result?

2. What was the basic content of the decree?

3. Look up the following scriptures to discern the importance of finding the decree.

   Daniel 6:12 and 15

   Esther 1:19

4. How did finding the decree, coupled with the fact that the law of the Medes and Persians could not be changed, affect the exiles?

5. Record how God unexpectedly intervened to help His people in the following scriptures.

   Genesis 22:9-14

Daniel 3:24-27

Matthew 2:13

6. What do the following scriptures tell us about God's intervention?

   Psalm 77:14-15

   Psalm 113:7-8

   Isaiah 44:24-26

MEMORY CHALLENGE

Psalm 37:6

He will make your righteousness shine like the dawn, the justice of your cause like the noonday sun.

(NIV)

Ezra 5 ended with the request by Tattenai and his associates that a search be made in the royal archives of Babylon to see if King Cyrus issued a decree to rebuild the Temple. Decrees were not all centralized in that day. Babylon held something like the central library of records including decrees; other areas were like branch libraries that might contain some records. The records had not been reorganized since the line of Cyrus had shifted to the line of Darius in 521 B.C. Finding a decree might be very difficult.

Ecbatana was the capital of the old Median Empire. It was a fortress used by the Persian kings as a summer residence because of its pleasant location and climate. In Ecbatana, papyrus and leather scrolls were kept instead of clay tablets because at 6,000 feet elevation the air was less hot and humid than in Babylon. The search was very thorough to go so far as to look in Ecbatana, but Darius so desired it, and it was done.

When the decree was finally discovered, it was wonderful for the exiles because it gave them permission to rebuild. Before, the enemies had tried to discourage, distract, and stop the rebuilding and had succeeded. But this time God had something unexpected planned in the form of a leather scroll in Ecbatana. The law of the Medes and Persians could not be changed. Therefore, not only did Darius have to support this rebuilding project, but he had to order Tattenai to do so as well. God had changed opposition to support.

This is a repeated pattern of the way God works. He intervenes in the lives of His people in unexpected ways. Just when it appears that another problem has presented itself and frustrations increase, He makes himself known in a way we would least expect.

Little fifth grader Johnny came to his mother with a problem one day after school. He wanted to play football with the other boys during recess, but the kids were rather selective about who could play, and Johnny was not included. His mother suggested all sorts of ideas such as boldly asking to play, having the playground instructor intervene, telling the classroom teacher, getting some of his other buddies to start another game, or just jumping into the game. None of these solutions were satisfactory to Johnny, but he really wanted to play.

"Well, son, I don't know what to tell you to do. But let's write this down in your prayer book you made in Sunday School and ask God to intervene," she suggested.

Several days later Johnny came home from school telling his mother about some of the good plays he had made in football. She was stunned and asked him if he was playing with the other boys at recess now. Johnny assured her that he was, and she wanted to know what had happened.

He told her, "I took my ball to school in my backpack one day, and when they didn't have a ball I said they could play with mine as long as I could play. Then they found out how good I was, and I play every day now."

The mother was just amazed. Who but God would have ever thought of that solution?But she was not surprised when she realized it was simply another case of God intervening in unexpected ways.

To conclude today's study, spend a moment asking the Holy Spirit to bring to your mind a personal situation where God intervened unexpectedly. Make a note of it below, and if you feel comfortable, be prepared to share this with your group.

MEMORY CHALLENGE

Write out Psalm 37:6 two or three times as preparation for memorizing it this week.

Cease Interference

Read Ezra 6:6-7.

1. Who is speaking in Ezra 6:6-7?

2. What does he basically say?

3. Like Tattenai, we sometimes think we know how things should be without checking with God. By doing this, do we ever interfere with God's plans? Summarize the following scriptures to help with your answer.

   1 Samuel 12:13-15; 13:11-14 (If you do not understand the significance of this event, try to discover it in a Bible commentary or ask in your small group.)

   Jonah 1:1-3

   John 8:3-11

4. In the example of the woman caught in adultery, the teachers of the law believed they knew the answer: stone her. But Christ had a different idea: forgive her. Are we ever guilty of believing we know what someone else should do because we know the rules, but really interfere with God because we do not know what He plans?

5. Using the following three scenarios as case studies of someone in the fellowship, think of the reaction of (1) yourself, (2) the Christian community, and then (3) what God might intend.

   • A young woman becomes pregnant without being married.

   • A young man has been diagnosed with cancer but has chosen not to have the radiation treatment.

   • A couple who is able financially has chosen not to help an elderly parent who appears to be in need.

6. Should we as Christians be very cautious about interfering with someone else's life until we consult God about His plan?

7. Instead of interfering, what might be a better plan? Record the following scriptures to help with your answer.

   Philippians 4:6

   1 Timothy 2:1

   James 1:5-8

Tattenai must have been shocked to receive Darius's answer, which was to cease interfering! He was probably expecting some praise for informing the new king of this danger but instead was told to stay out of it! What Tattenai thought would happen ended up not happening at all.

That may also be true in our lives. Because of our backgrounds or our beliefs about certain issues, we sometimes think we know what should happen. Sometimes we try to make it happen! But then God comes along and tells us not to interfere because He has a different plan. God's ways are not always our ways. Being a true and sincere follower means we are open to recognizing new ways of doing things and allowing God to work.

"For my thoughts are not your thoughts, neither are your ways my ways," declares the Lord. "As the heavens are higher than the earth, so are my ways higher than your ways and my thoughts than your thoughts" (Isaiah 55:8-9).

How will our righteousness or justice ever shine?

Charge

Read Ezra 6:8-12.

1. Darius gave Tattenai three responsibilities to help the Jews. List these.

2. What was to be the punishment if Tattenai or anyone else did not carry out this charge?

3. According to verse 10, why did Darius want the exiles to be helped in rebuilding the Temple?

4. Why would Darius care if these Jewish exiles prayed for him? If necessary, look back to Lesson 1, Day One, and review the theology of Cyrus, whom Darius followed.

5. According to verse 12, what did Darius say God had done?

6. Summarize the following scriptures, which also refer to God as the One who caused His name to dwell in the Temple.

   Deuteronomy 12:4-5, 11

   1 Kings 9:2-3

Not only was Tattenai told not to interfere with the rebuilding of the Temple, but he was charged with the responsibilities of paying expenses from the treasury, supplying animals for the sacrifices, and praying for the well-being of the king. This hurt not only his pride but his pocketbook as well!

And Darius was serious. When he had conquered Babylon, he impaled 3,000 rebellious Babylonians to help secure his throne. He meant for Tattenai and company to cooperate.

Part of Darius's motive in all this was to be prayed for and receive the blessings of another "god." If he helped God succeed, then he believed he would be rewarded.

But God is perfectly capable of making His name dwell wherever He chooses. In the Old Testament it resided in His Temple, but with the coming of Christ it resides in our beings as we choose to be called by His Name. What does it mean to be called by His name?

The story is told of a little boy, Timmy, who was roller-blading in his neighborhood park. He hadn't worn his knee or elbow pads that day, although he knew his mother would be angry if she found out. But he was skillful and hardly ever fell down, so Timmy felt sure that his mom would never know.

Unfortunately, he took a corner blocked by trees at breakneck speed and collided with a young man jogging with his dog. Except for a shin bruise where Timmy had hit him, the young man was fine. Timmy was another story. Both knees and one elbow lost so much skin it looked like he needed grafting. Of course it stung unmercifully and bled profusely. But it was probably going to hurt more when he got home and was grounded from rollerblading. Timmy was in both physical and emotional pain.

But the young man was so kind and gentle. Instead of being angry with Timmy for being so reckless, he picked him up and ran to his car for his first-aid kit. He gave Timmy a cool drink of water and then cleaned all his wounds with hydrogen peroxide. When he applied the peroxide he blew on the wound to keep it from stinging so much. Then he bandaged Timmy and helped him up. The young man offered to accompany Timmy home and be a support when he faced his mother. Finally, he asked if they could be friends and got the permission of Timmy's mother to come back the next day and take him for an ice cream cone.

As the young man was leaving Timmy's house, Timmy stopped him by tugging on his sleeve. "Mister, are you Jesus?"

"No," the young man smiled. "I'm just called by His name."

God can dwell in a building and did dwell in the Temple. But God also dwells in the lives of His believers who are called by His name.

Either write Psalm 37:6 several times (on a separate sheet) or recite it aloud, whichever is most effective for you.

Correction

Read Ezra 6:13-14.

1. In a quick review, match the people to their role in helping God's plan come together.

   Zerubbabel — Governor of Trans-Euphrates who was corrected by Darius to help the Jewish exiles rebuild

   Darius — Prophets who challenged the people to get on with rebuilding the Temple

   Haggai and Zechariah — King who searched for the decree of Cyrus and followed up on it

   Tattenai — Jewish elder in charge of the Temple project

2. With the above roles and today's scripture as an aid, write a paragraph about how God brought a plan together to get the Jewish exiles back to work rebuilding the Temple.

3. Summarize the following scriptures, which demonstrate how God's correction helps bring a plan together.

   Psalm 81:13-16

   Proverbs 16:20

   Jeremiah 10:23-25

4. Do we have the assurance that no plan can ever come against God's plan? Record Proverbs 21:30 here.

5. When it looks like God's plan will never come together, what does He promise us? (See Ephesians 3:20.)

A comedy adventure on television had the two good guys trying to set the world right for justice. While they had some experience in police work, they never seemed to have the information, tools, or correct location at the time they needed it. The show was a comedy of improvisation to beat the bad guys. As the adventure would proceed, one of the two good guys would say, "I love it when a plan comes together."

These two short verses of Ezra 6 demonstrate how God makes a plan come together. Haggai and Zechariah prophesied for God and corrected the people by exhorting them to refocus their priorities concerning rebuilding the Temple. Zerubbabel gave the lay leadership in the actual building process. The enemies, led by Tattenai, came forth again, but when they tried to get the king on their side, Tattenai and company were corrected. The government got behind the Jewish exiles and supported them with official sanction! Talk about a plan coming together!

Who would have ever believed a lost scroll in a pagan library in an outlying town would unexpectedly turn up and twist everything around? Suddenly God's people were in the driver's seat. They even got favored treatment from a pagan king. *The king's heart is in the hand of the LORD; he directs it like a watercourse wherever he pleases* (Proverbs 21:1).

I will go before thee, and make the crooked places straight: I will break in pieces the gates of brass, and cut in sunder the bars of iron (Isaiah 45:2, KJV). *Listen! I hear the voice of someone shouting, "Make a way for the Lord through the wilderness; make him a straight, smooth road throughout the desert. Fill the valleys; level the hills; straighten out the crooked paths and smooth off the rough spots in the road. The glory of the Lord will be seen by all mankind together."* The Lord *has spoken—it shall be* (Isaiah 40:3-5, TLB). Don't you love it when a plan comes together?

How does Psalm 37:6 relate to the idea in today's lesson of God's plan coming together?

Completion

Read Ezra 6:14-18.

1. Which emotion was present at the completion of the Temple (verse 16)?

2. When the Temple was dedicated, how many bulls, rams, male lambs, and male goats were sacrificed?

3. How does this compare to the first dedication? This information comes from 1 Kings 8:63.

4. Who are the priests and Levites spoken of in Ezra 6:18? (See Numbers 3:5-10.)

5. From your knowledge of Israel and the modern-day world, is the Temple the Jewish exiles rebuilt still there?

6. Will there ever be another Temple in Israel? (See Revelation 11:1, 19.)

7. Why will the final Temple be destroyed, and where will the new Temple be? Summarize the important points from Revelation 21:1-4, 22-23.

On March 12, 515 B.C., as prophesied by Jeremiah, the Temple was completed with great joy 70 years after its destruction. This meant the work was finished 21 years after the foundation was laid, but only 4½ years after Haggai and Zechariah exhorted the people to get back to work.

The Temple was not as lavish as the original, nor was the dedication. Solomon sacrificed 200 times as many oxen and sheep when he dedicated the first Temple. This time 712 animals were sacrificed, including a male goat for each tribe of Israel.

The sad news is that this was not the last time the Temple was destroyed. In A.D. 70 the Temple was once again destroyed by the Romans and has never been rebuilt. The Temple we read about in the New Testament, the one where Christ, Peter, Nicodemus, Stephen, and Paul worshiped, was the Temple these Jewish exiles built. The work done by Zerubbabel and supporters has never since been duplicated.

Revelation indicates that when the last days of the earth come, Israel will be a nation and they will have a Temple. Although Israel was overrun in A.D. 70 and was not recognized as a nation after that, 1,879 years later God performed one of His amazing completions when Israel was once again recognized as a nation in 1949. When the Temple will be rebuilt we do not know, but this must be done before Christ can come to gather His own to himself. At that time we are promised a new heaven and a new earth where the Temple will be the Lamb of God, Christ himself. We will not need a Temple because our dwelling will be in God. And there will be greater joy than we could ever imagine at the beautiful completion of God's amazing plan.

MEMORY CHALLENGE

When God's total plan comes together at the end of time, will justice and righteousness win out? Try to find a scripture to back up your answer.

Celebration

Read Ezra 6:19-22.

1. After the dedication of the Temple, what was the first celebration?

2. What is Passover? Read Exodus 12:1-20 and write a paragraph below explaining it.

3. Passover represents God's _____.

4. Had Passover always been celebrated from the time God commanded it during Moses' time until the exiles celebrated it on April 21, 515 B.C.? Summarize 2 Chronicles 29:1-11 and 2 Chronicles 29:35—30:1.

5. Why would this Passover be such a special celebration?

6. How had the Lord filled the people with joy according to verse 22?

Imagine yourself in a situation where you had been away from home for a long time. Maybe you were gone during World War II, were a missionary in a foreign country, or simply went away to college without getting back home for quite a while. It's Christmastime, and this year you are making the long trek back to be with loved ones and celebrate the most significant holiday of the year for you. Can you feel the anticipation, the excitement, the joy?

This is how the exiles felt when Passover arrived five weeks after the dedication of the Temple. They were home at last in Jerusalem with a Temple in which to celebrate this most important holiday. It had been 70 years since this occurred, and they were filled with joy!

Two groups of Jews were present. There were the exiles who had returned and those already living in the land who had stayed. Some were Jews, but others were heathen and could participate in Passover if they agreed to adhere to the Jewish law.

The Levites acted as heads of families and slaughtered the Passover lambs for both laity, who might be unclean, and priests, who had too many other duties. Then they followed the law by celebrating the Feast of Unleavened Bread for seven days.

They celebrated being home in Jerusalem; they celebrated having the Temple completed; they celebrated Passover; and they celebrated the Lord changing the attitude of the king so that all this could be completed. Most of all, they celebrated life and the One who gives it. They celebrated God the King.

MEMORY CHALLENGE

Write Psalm 37:6 from memory below. Go back and review the entire psalm by trying to recite it to yourself.

Ezra

■ A study of Ezra 7

LESSON **7**

Ezra

Read Ezra 7:1-10.

1. How far can Ezra's lineage be traced back?

2. Read Exodus 40:12-16 to learn the background to Question 1 and summarize.

3. Phinehas in this genealogy was also very important to Ezra's background. What did he do, and what was he promised according to Numbers 25:10-13?

4. How is Ezra described in Ezra 7:6a and 10?

5. List the three specific things to which Ezra devoted himself according to verse 10.

6. Are we admonished to follow these three observances of Ezra? Record the following verses to help you with your answer.

   Deuteronomy 11:18-19

   Psalm 119:129-130

   Proverbs 24:3-4

   2 Timothy 2:15

7. What special favor from God did Ezra have according to verse 6 and 9?

8. Is the hand of God in this context mentioned elsewhere in the Bible? Look up these scriptures and record.

   Genesis 49:24

   2 Chronicles 6:4

After Ezra 6, there is 58-year period of silence explained in Ezra 7 by the phrase *after these things*. During this time the events of the book of Esther took place in Babylon. In Jerusalem the excitement of the Temple completion had worn off. Nothing was being done to rebuild Jerusalem's walls or gates. The people were farming the land, enjoying their own homes and the Temple worship. They were beginning to compromise the separateness from the Gentiles around them and were intermarrying. The Law was being neglected and not taught. The excitement was gone.

Also evident in the first sentence of Ezra 7 is the reign of a new king, Artaxerxes. Darius had been most successful during his reign and brought many territories under his domain. He was a capable administrator who organized his empire in satraps, or provinces. Each had a governor appointed by Darius to whom local government was responsible.

Darius was succeeded by his son Xerxes I, who is named Ahasuerus in the Bible. He reigned 22 years before being assassinated; he was succeeded to the throne by Artaxerxes I, his younger son. Artaxerxes had killed the rightful heir, and under his leadership the Persian Empire began to slowly crumble.

This is the point at which Ezra entered the scene. He was held in high esteem by King Artaxerxes and may have had a position of leadership such as "Secretary of Jewish Affairs." He desired to return to Jerusalem, feeling God was calling him to fulfill a need there. He must have requested permission to return and was rewarded with something like a letter of recommendation outlining all the conditions of his return.

Ezra had studied and prepared for his moment in history. He believed it was not enough just to study, but one must also obey the Word. To simply study would be like seeing *through a glass, darkly* (1 Corinthians 13:12, KJV). Neither did he believe it was enough to obey without studying. What if one obeyed the wrong teaching? Finally, when he did study to know the Word and then obey it, Ezra felt it was his responsibility to teach it to others. So Ezra's job was to be priest now that the Temple was built. He hoped to call the people back to study and obedience and put some enthusiasm in their spiritual lives. Ezra was faithful to this calling and therefore *the hand of the LORD his God was on him* (verse 6).

MEMORY CHALLENGE

Write out Psalm 37:18 two or three times as preparation for memorizing it this week.

Expedition

Read Ezra 7:11-26, concentrating on verses 11-14.

1. How is Ezra described in verses 11-12?

2. We, too, are to be familiar with the Lord's law. Turn to Psalm 19:7-11 and list the different names used for the law. Then record the phrases showing its benefits.

3. The word "study" that is often used in context with Ezra's work on the scriptures means "to seek." What does 2 Chronicles 12:14 tell us we will do if we do not seek God and His Word?

4. How is Artaxerxes described in Ezra 7:12?

5. Look up Daniel 2:37 and find the two phrases that are similar to Ezra 7:11-12.

6. Who was given permission to return to Israel in verse 13?

7. Who gave permission besides the king in verse 14?

8. Who were these men? Look up Esther 1:14.

Ezra requested permission to go on a teaching mission to Jerusalem and was rewarded with a letter of recommendation by Artaxerxes for the expedition. This was like a passport for Ezra and fellow Israelites as they passed through different kingdoms along the way. The letter held the full authority of the king and his seven advisers who performed a function similar to our Supreme Court. Later verses of Ezra 7 will discuss the conveying of gifts from the treasury and further responsibilities of Ezra.

Why would the king be so generous with Ezra? Obviously Ezra was in the king's favor, for the descriptions of Ezra in the letter are complimentary. But we must also keep in mind the polytheism of Artaxerxes. Probably the law of Moses had been brought to Babylon with the early captives and handed down in the Jewish community. Otherwise, Ezra would not have been so well-versed. The Babylonian captors had most likely confiscated their own copy and read it. They wanted to record what other people believed about their gods so they would have political and military advantages through understanding of the culture. Also, a polytheist wants to please every god.

The king's letter opened the door for any Jewish exile to go on this expedition, but only 2,000 chose to go with Ezra. The trip took four months but was made easier by the king's letter, which was Ezra's blessing.

Write out Psalm 37:18 below.

Elements

Read Ezra 7:15-20.

1. King Artaxerxes gave the Israelites permission to take elements of support from three sources. What were these (verses 15-16)?

2. What were the Jews to do with these elements (verses 17-18)?

3. If other resources were needed, from where were they to come (verse 20)?

4. What Ezra and fellow exiles were given permission to do sounds very similar to the commands given by the Lord in Deuteronomy 12:4-14. Read this passage and record the main points.

5. These elements of gold, silver, and offerings given the Jews were representative of their faith to make this journey, not knowing what was really involved. What are our elements of faith? Begin your own list and then add to it by looking up the following scriptures.

Romans 5:1-3

Hebrews 11:1-2, 13-16

Ezra and his fellow exiles were not to leave Babylon empty-handed. First, they were to have the gold and silver from the king and his seven advisers. It is believed these were utensils from the Temple that were not returned with the first set of exiles. The king was freely giving them as a gift to Ezra's God of heaven. Then the returning Jews were to ask remaining Jews if they would like to contribute to the support of this expedition. This was a repeat of the experience of the first group of exiles as recorded in Ezra 1:6. Finally, the royal treasury was to be opened for additional needs. As a good polytheist, Artaxerxes also stipulated that the funds be used for the sacrifices necessary to worship.

We, too, have elements of faith as we journey through life. By faith we receive joy, peace, grace, and mercy. We walk in the light even when we cannot see where we are going. We believe God will fulfill His promises to us even when we see no hope. We experience His love through our faith, and no one can ever take that from us. We are confident because we know by our faith who is in control.

Jean's parents divorced when she was a little girl because her father was an alcoholic. An aunt who loved the Lord took her to church, and she accepted Christ at the age of 16. At that point, Jean began to pray for her parents.

Her mother gave her heart to the Lord a few years later, but her father continued his wayward lifestyle for another 20 years. In the meantime, Jean married and had children of her own, but she never stopped praying for her dad and his salvation.

Jean's father eventually ended up on skid row in Kansas City, and one night, after realizing he had used all his human resources, he went into a rescue mission and gave his heart to Christ. He was gradually able to put his life back together. He quit drinking, got a job, eventually remarried, and began to call Jean and be a part of her life. He wasn't perfect, but he was definitely a changed man. He even began to raise an orphan boy to make up, some believe, for the fact that he was never there for Jean.

Jean could have given up, but she had faith. She believed in what she hoped for and did not see, not because of herself, but because she served a great God. These were her elements of faith and by exercising them she was able to see her father brought to the Lord.

MEMORY CHALLENGE

Whose days are known to the Lord?

Extravagance

Read Ezra 7:21-24.

1. Does it sound as if the king is being extravagant with the Jews?

2. Does God give us only what we need, or is He extravagant? Summarize the following scriptures to help with your answer.

   Job 42:10, 12-15

   Luke 5:4-7

   John 6:12-13

   Romans 5:5

   In *The Message*, Romans 5:5 reads, *We can't round up enough containers to hold everything God generously pours into our lives through the Holy Spirit!*

3. How does God encourage us to be extravagant with Him? (See John 12:3-7.)

4. How is God extravagant with us?

   Psalm 103:3-6

   Malachi 3:10-12

   Romans 8:2, 15-17

   Ephesians 3:20

The king was very generous with Ezra and the returning Jews. He recognized their service to the community and was willing to support it. This is the first known record of government exempting Temple workers from paying taxes. In our culture today, nonprofit organizations such as the church are still not required to pay taxes.

God was generous to His people through the king. He continues to be extravagant with us as we allow Him to work in our lives.

MEMORY CHALLENGE

Fill in the blanks: "The _____ of the _____ are _____ to the LORD, and their _____ will _____ _____." Psalm 37:_____

Exhortation

Read Ezra 7:25-26.

1. What assignment did King Artaxerxes give Ezra in verse 25?

2. Ezra would have been very familiar with this idea, for he knew the law of Moses. Summarize the following scriptures.

   Exodus 18:20-23

   Deuteronomy 16:18

3. What was to happen if the people were not obedient to what Ezra taught them (verse 26)?

4. Read Psalm 52 and record what will happen to the evil man as opposed to the man who chooses to obey the law of the Lord.

   Evil Man   *Obedient Man*

Ezra was given quite a serious charge by the king to exhort the laws of the kingdom of God. *Guideposts Family Concordance* defines "exhortation" as "encouraging others to commendable conduct." In the context of Ezra 7, it seems that "exhortation" meant more than just encouragement. Webster's definition of "admonition" seems to be more appropriate. Anytime people are told they will be banished, imprisoned, have all their property confiscated, or be put to death, it seems they are being more than just "encouraged" to be good!

We live in a day where many countries make laws but then only "slap hands" when the laws are broken. King Artaxerxes was serious about lawbreakers. He wanted Ezra to see that the laws of his kingdom were obeyed, and men prosecuted and punished who did not follow the law. He gave Ezra a way to set up this judicial system and expected him to follow it. Furthermore, he wanted Ezra to have full power to include the laws of Ezra's God in all this.

The Church is a reflection of society in many ways. We as Christians can be apathetic about lawbreakers. We may know of someone in the church, claiming to follow Christ, who is living a sinful or evil lifestyle. We often feel it's not "our place" to confront them; yet it seems the caring and mature thing to do. We exhort not to condemn but to give one an opportunity to repent and turn from evil.

If your brother sins against you, go and show him his fault, just between the two of you. If he listens to you, you have won your brother over. But if he will not listen, take one or two others along, so that "every matter may be established by the testimony of two or three witnesses." If he refuses to listen to them, tell it to the church; and if he refuses to listen even to the church, treat him as you would a pagan or a tax collector (Matthew 18:15-17).

The purpose of exhortation is for repentance. While in Ezra's day the punishment was swift, in our day sometimes it is slow. We can live many years in our sin before our lives or the lives of our families fall apart. We may live many years before we die and must face our Creator, who does not take sin lightly. Not having immediate consequences makes it easier for us to continue in our sin and never face it.

Ezra gives us a wonderful model of being wise and well-versed about the Law by teaching it to others, and then by obeying it. Maybe we have loved ones that the Lord would lay on our hearts to remind of this truth today. Exhorting them in love may save them from many painful consequences.

MEMORY CHALLENGE

Today we studied the obedient man. What will happen with the inheritance of the blameless?

Exiled No More

Read Ezra 7:27-28.

1. In verse 27, Ezra begins writing in the first person. He uses first person for the remainder of the book of Ezra, with the exception of two verses in chapter 8 (verses 35-36). After beginning to write in first person, what is the first thing Ezra does?

2. After a week's study of the Word, let us pause and take some moments to praise or bless God. Record the following scriptures.

   2 Samuel 22:1-4

   1 Chronicles 16:23-25

   Psalm 103:1-2

3. David gave a wonderful example of praise in 1 Chronicles 29:10-13. Record the main points below.

4. Ezra does not take credit for the good favor he has received from the king. Instead, he gives the credit to God. Is this scriptural? Summarize the following verses.

   Exodus 3:19-20

   Proverbs 21:1

5. Because the hand of God was upon Ezra, he took courage. If we are children of God, walking in His way and being open to correction, His hand is upon us as well. He also provides ways for us to develop courage. Record the following scriptures.

   Psalm 27:14

   Isaiah 43:3

   1 John 3:21

Because of Ezra's courage, he and 2,000 other Jews would be exiled no more. When we live in fear, we exile ourselves. We are afraid to become the people God intends us to be because we won't risk, learn, grow, examine, think, question, challenge, or change. *By entering through faith into what God has always wanted to do for us—set us right with him, make us fit for him—we have it all together with God because of our Master Jesus. And that's not all: We throw open our doors to God and discover at the same moment that he has already thrown open his door to us. We find ourselves standing where we always hoped we might stand—out in the wide open spaces of God's grace and glory, standing tall and shouting our praise* (Romans 5:1-2, TM).

"Fear not" appears in the Bible at least 63 times. God does not intend for us to live this way, but to live in faith believing that He is in control. *Being confident of this, that he who began a good work in you will carry it on to completion until the day of Christ Jesus* (Philippians 1:6). We don't need to be exiled! We can have the confidence and courage of Ezra.

A young mother and her five-year-old daughter were driving home at dusk on a highway when she realized she had a flat tire. First she looked for a flashlight knowing it would be dark soon, but there was none. Knowing she would have to hurry to have enough light, she opened the trunk to find the jack. It was there, but this was a foreign car and the jack was unlike any she had ever seen. She couldn't figure out how to use it. She decided to begin loosening the lug nuts on the wheel, but she was pregnant and soon discovered she did not have the strength required for this task.

At this point she realized she was not going to be able to change this tire. "Lord, I can't do this, and I don't want to be stranded on this highway after dark with my daughter. Would You send someone to help me?" she prayed.

In a matter of minutes a clean-cut young man stopped and offered his services to change the tire. He explained the reason he stopped. He recognized her car because he was her paper boy. Ten minutes later, the mother and daughter were on their way home, safe and sound.

The point of the story is that when the young mother knew she was out of her own resources, she had confidence in the One with infinite resources. She did not need to fear but took courage knowing the problem was God's because she was His child. She wouldn't have to be exiled for long on that highway. She had faith, believing her life was in God's hands.

MEMORY CHALLENGE

Review Psalm 37:7.

Ezra

■ A study of Ezra 8

DAY ONE

Genealogy and Geography

Read all of Ezra 8. Today's study will be on verses 1-15.

1. Write down the names from the genealogy that you recognize from elsewhere in the Bible.

2. Write down any family names that appear to be the same as in Ezra 2:3-15.

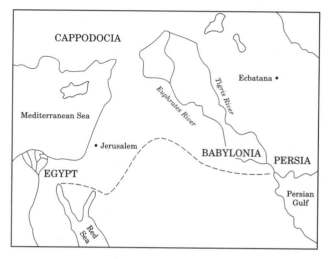

3. Locate Persia and Babylonia on your map. What two main rivers run through them?

4. These two rivers are the headwaters of the earth. Record the main points from Genesis 2:10-14.

The genealogy of those who left begins with the members of the priestly tribe and Davidic families. In every case except Joab those returning were only from families whose descendants had returned 80 years before. Their genealogy is found in Ezra 2:3-15. Phinehas, David, Jonathan, and Joab are well-known men from earlier in Hebrew history. The names of Daniel and the two Zechariahs are not the same people with whom we are familiar.

Because in Lesson 2 an entire week's study was devoted to genealogy, we are going to digress. A genealogy is a map of family lineage. We are going to pause to look at a geographic map to find the places we have been studying in the book of Ezra.

MEMORY CHALLENGE

Psalm 37:19

*In times of disaster
they will not wither;
in days of famine
they will enjoy plenty.*

(NIV)

5. In Jeremiah 51:13 God is speaking to the people of Babylon through Jeremiah of the Tigris and Euphrates Rivers. What does He say?

6. Locate Jerusalem on your map and make the dotted line a solid line to indicate the journey of Ezra and the exiles.

7. Locate Ecbatana on the map. What have we learned happened here?

8. Find the Ahava Canal and Casiphia mentioned in Ezra 8:15.

Question 8 was a trick question, for the locations of the Ahava Canal and Casiphia are unknown. Genealogy and geography certainly don't bring us any major insights about our relationship with God. However, learning background information helps us to seek the big picture, which then allows us to stand amazed at how God brings it all together.

MEMORY CHALLENGE

Review Psalm 37:19.

DAY TWO

Gathered

Read Ezra 8:15-20.

1. How many days did the exiles camp at the Ahava Canal?

2. While the exiles were gathered at the camp, Ezra became aware of a problem. What was it?

3. What action did Ezra take?

4. How did this problem work out?

5. Ezra was missing some important players on his team, so he went out and recruited. Are we important players on God's team? Are we ever missing from the "gathering"? Summarize the following scriptures.

   Genesis 4:13

   Jonah 1:1-3

   Luke 18:22-23

6. Record the following Scriptures that teach us about our role on God's team.

   Isaiah 43:10

   Ephesians 4:1-3

1 Peter 4:10

While the group was gathered at the river, Ezra noticed there were no Levites present. He realized this problem would greatly hamper his program in Jerusalem. Why did they not come? First, the Levites were comfortable in Babylon where they were settled as teachers of the Law. Also, the best Levitical positions in Jerusalem were already taken by the earlier group led back by Zerubbabel. But again, God's hand was working, and he gathered 38 Levites led by Sherebiah, Hashabiah, and Jeshaiah. Also, 220 Temple servants called Nethinims joined the party.

God had put the Levites in a special position in His Body. But in this situation they had an opportunity to use their God-given gifts, and they chose not to do so. That left a gap in God's work, which made the whole system break down. In order to help God's plan come together, we must fulfill the roles He gives us!

When Wisdom of the Word was attempting to start a Bible study at Mable Bassett Correctional Facility, the leader needed a partner. For a long while no one came forward, until one of the ladies, Marie, realized she could not get away from Matthew 25:36, which says, *I was in prison and you came to visit me.* She said she knew nothing about inmates and didn't know if she could relate at all, but she felt led to go.

The first day she walked into the chapel at the prison, a young woman was sitting alone on the couch crying. The love in Marie's heart helped her to walk right over to this convicted criminal, sit down beside her, and ask what was wrong. That day was the young woman's grandmother's funeral, and she had not been given permission to go. Marie empathized, prayed, and cared. She was just what the inmate needed. Marie might not have felt up to the task, but before she was there five minutes the Lord had used her to be the one to gather, stand in the gap, and minister. Someone needed to fulfill this role, and by being obedient, she was used mightily.

MEMORY CHALLENGE

What will happen to the blameless in times of disaster?

God's Protection

Read Ezra 8:21-23.

1. Why did Ezra proclaim a fast?

2. Is humbling ourselves, praying, and fasting a pattern God is showing us to secure His protection?

   2 Chronicles 20:3-4

   2 Chronicles 7:14

   Esther 4:15-16

   Psalm 35:13-14

   Acts 13:3

3. Why was Ezra embarrassed to ask the king for a military escort on this dangerous journey?

4. Ezra's faith in God's protection was put to the test. Read Psalm 91 and record the major points about God's protection.

5. We are assured the Lord's hand is on us if we look to Him, but what happens to those who forsake Him (verse 22)?

6. The above idea is reiterated in the following scriptures. Summarize them below.

    2 Chronicles 15:1-2

    Psalm 34:16

7. Today we can fast for specific needs. Can you remember a particular time when you fasted? What was the reason? What was the outcome? If you feel comfortable, share this with your group.

Ezra proclaimed God's protection to the king, but then he realized he should not take that for granted. A 900-mile trip lay ahead in the western part of the empire, which was much less stable than central Persia. Ambush and robbery were very real threats along the way, and Ezra remembered they would be carrying gold, silver, and bronze.

In primitive cultures, food preparation was quite time-consuming, so declaring a fast meant there would be extra time to pray. It would represent the Jews' dependence on God for protection. For Ezra and the exiles it was effective, for there were no incidents along the way and they arrived with all goods intact. God's call through Ezra to fast in the face of serious danger brought God's protection.

MEMORY CHALLENGE

What will happen to the blameless in times of famine?

Guard Carefully

Read Ezra 8:24-30.

1. Who did Ezra set apart to carry the gold and silver articles?

2. How many talents of silver and silver articles was each of these 24 men responsible for? If 26 talents equals one ton in weight, how many tons was each man responsible for? What are your ideas about how this would be possible? Remember that this does not include the gold.

3. Ezra told the 24 men, "You as well as these articles are _____ to the LORD." What do the following scriptures tell us about consecration?

   Leviticus 22:1-3

   Isaiah 52:11

4. What are the three key words Ezra says to the 24 men in verse 29?

5. Do we guard carefully what is most sacred to God? In this situation, the articles for the Temple were most sacred to God. Look up the following scriptures and record them. Then decide what we have that is most sacred to God.

Psalm 73:1

Proverbs 4:23

Matthew 5:8

1 Thessalonians 3:13

Our_____ is most sacred to God.

6. How do we guard our hearts? Record the following scriptures.

   Deuteronomy 26:16

   Proverbs 3:5

   Matthew 22:37

   1 Peter 3:15

These 24 men were assigned to carry $4,500,000 worth of articles for God's Temple. No wonder Ezra wanted everyone to pray and fast! If bandits were indeed plentiful, they certainly had something worth being concerned about. Ezra said, "Guard them carefully!"

But our hearts are more precious to God than any of the gold, silver, or bronze articles. He wants us to guard them carefully. We live in a world full of evil, and this must be a daily task.

Scott Simpson is a pro golfer on the PGA tour. He is a fine Christian gentleman who is known for his witness. Several years ago he was being interviewed after winning a big tournament. While he spoke some about golf, the thrust of his words were about God.

In those circumstances he confessed that it was hard to remain humble and realize that he was just an ordinary person and that God should be the real focus of our admiration and love. He is the one to be lifted up and praised and receive the glory, not a pro golfer. Scott said he had to work hard every day to remember he was no more special than anyone else. He said he had to guard his heart carefully.

It's true, isn't it? We do something well, and our pride swells. We do something special, and we think we're special. We live around evil, and we become tempted with it. We take a vacation from our spirituality for a few weeks, and we stumble. Yes, the condition of our hearts is precarious. We must not take it for granted, but guard it well.

MEMORY CHALLENGE

Fill in the blanks:
"In_____ of _____
they will not_____; in
_____of _____ they
will _____ _____ ."

Psalm _____:_____

DAY FIVE

Good Hand

Read Ezra 8:31-34.

1. According to Ezra 8:31, why was the gathering not attacked along the way by bandits and enemies?

2. How many days did the exiles rest after they got to Jerusalem?

3. What happened on the fourth day?

4. Was everything accounted for?

5. The good hand of God truly was upon Ezra and company. How is the good hand of God upon us? Jot down a few ideas and then record the following scriptures for additional ideas.

Exodus 34:6-7

Psalm 139:10

Psalm 145:16

John 10:27-30

The journey of these exiles was fraught with problems. In the lesson this week it has already been mentioned that the exiles traveled 900 miles in undeveloped areas where bandits were plentiful. The group, which included women, children, and animals, averaged only seven miles a day. Also, the weight of the precious objects was a problem; the gold, silver, and bronze weighed close to 29 tons. Have you ever wondered how only 2,000 men transported all that weight? Technically, if 24 men were responsible for the gold, silver, and bronze, each was in charge of 2,400 pounds! Surely they had the help of animals, but how many animals would it take to carry 2,400 pounds? It's doubtful that one man could even keep his eye on all the animals under his responsibility.

Yet in verse 34 we read that every single item was accounted for. Nothing was lost, stolen, borrowed, or damaged. It was all there. Surely this was God's doing. Surely He intended not an article to be harmed. Who could question that through dangerous territory, with so many items of value that weighed so much and were so difficult to transport, that it was God's doing not to have a single loss? Surely the good hand of God was upon the exiles.

MEMORY CHALLENGE

Psalm 37:19 says, *In times of disaster they will not wither; in days of famine they will enjoy plenty.* How does this relate to the study today concerning the good hand of God being upon us?

Goats and Governors

Read Ezra 8:35-36.

1. After the three days of rest, the exiles weighed the sacred articles and then took two more actions (verses 35 and 36). What were these two actions?

2. What happened after the king's orders were delivered to the governors?

3. What were the two types of offerings sacrificed?

4. Look up in a dictionary or concordance the definition of "offering."

5. One definition of "offering" is "a voluntary act of worship that represents consecration of the worshiper to God." What happened after the first burnt offering recorded in Scripture occurred? (Read Genesis 8:20.)

6. What are some other offerings with which God is pleased?

   Romans 12:1

   In *The Message* this is translated, *So here's what I want you to do, God helping you: Take your everyday ordinary life—your sleeping, eating, going-to-work, and walking-around life—and place it before God as an offering.*

2 Timothy 4:6-7

Hebrews 13:15-16

God is very pleased with us when we give of ourselves
to Him in consecrated worship. In this way our lives
become an offering. Rebecca Manley Pippert tells the
story of a young nurse whose life was an offering.

One of the nurse's patients was a helpless woman who
had suffered a cerebral aneurysm. She could not talk
and had no control over her body. The other nurses
said that she had no awareness of her surroundings,
and caring for her was a difficult task they avoided.

But the young nurse sang to her, talked to her, and
smiled at her even though she received no response.
On Thanksgiving Day the nurse was called in to work
because they were shorthanded. There she was, caring
for this woman when she wanted to be home eating a
turkey dinner. But she determined to make her life an
offering even when the circumstances were less than
desirable. The nurse told her patient it was Thanksgiving and she had been in a bad mood because she
wanted to be home, but now that she was caring for
her she was thankful and happy she could help her on
this special day.

The other nurses were wrong. The patient *was* aware,
for when the young nurse spoke those words to her,
tears trickled down her cheek. One nurse's life was an
offering; it was a consecration of living for the worship
of God, and it had touched the life of one helpless
woman.

MEMORY CHALLENGE

Write Psalm 37:19 in the space below.

Ezra

LESSON 9

■ **A study of Ezra 9**

DAY ONE

Apart

Read Ezra 9, concentrating on verses 1-2.

1. In verses 1-2, the leaders went to Ezra with a problem. What was it?

2. Why was the above answer a problem? Look up the following scriptures and summarize them to help with your answer.

    Exodus 34:11-16

    Deuteronomy 7:1-5

    Judges 3:5-6

3. God's people were to be set apart. They could be set apart only if they_____

    _____.

    To help fill in the blank with your own words, read Leviticus 18:26a.

4. Those who have studied under Jeannie McCullough's ministry in Wisdom of the Word know she calls this _____
    _____. Record the following scriptures.

    Exodus 19:5

    Deuteronomy 11:26-28

    Jeremiah 42:6

    John 14:15

MEMORY CHALLENGE

Psalm 37:23

*If the LORD delights
in a man's way,
he makes his steps firm.*

(NIV)

5. It is possible that there were not many copies of the Law. Ezra was well-versed in the Law, but those living in Jerusalem who returned with Zerubbabel may not have been as familiar with it. Read 2 Kings 22:8–23:3 and tell how it relates to this theory.

6. Is ignorance an excuse for disobedience? Should the Jerusalem Jews at least have been aware that God had commanded them to be a people set apart? Why? The following scriptures should help with your answer.

    Joshua 23:12-13

    1 Kings 11:1-2

7. Does it sound possible that part of the reason the children of Israel had lost their land in the first place was because they allowed other nations to infiltrate their land and lives?

Seventy-five years after Zerubbabel and the first group of captives returned to Jerusalem, Ezra arrived with his 2,000. He believed he left captivity to return to the Holy Land and was anxious to be a part of the group of holy people set apart. Ezra saw that the Temple was rebuilt but was possibly disappointed to discover the walls of the city were still in disrepair.

When Ezra had been in Jerusalem for 4 and a half months, some leaders approached him and pointed out that the people had intermarried with the nations around them—the very nations from whom God told them to be set apart. Being a student of the Law, Ezra recognized this as disobedience and knew this was one of the very reasons the children of Israel had lost their land in the first place. He knew that God had commanded His people to be set apart in order to avoid idolatry and immorality. Ezra was appalled at the situation.

It is possible that copies of the Law were not plentiful and that the Jerusalem Jews had not been instructed in it. They should have known from their history that they were being disobedient, but often when instruction is not kept in front of us we do not take it seriously. The old saying "out of sight, out of mind" fits here. Perhaps this is why Ezra was called to Jerusalem at this time to be the teacher of the Law.

Ezra worked in Jerusalem for 15 years. Ezra 9 records one segment of his work as he taught the people and tried to reform them. Nehemiah 8 records one of Ezra's efforts at teaching the Law, and it may relate to this very episode.

Earlier in the book of Ezra we read of disappointment. Often during times of disappointment, we let down and do things we shouldn't. Have you ever felt a little down because of disappointment and ended up buying a new outfit you could not afford or going to the kitchen to make a big hot fudge sundae you didn't need to eat? That is what these exiles, who became citizens of the Holy Land, did. They disregarded what they thought was best for them and what God had instructed them to do in order to make themselves feel better for the moment. Appeasement of the moment often carries consequences in the long run. What would happen if they were no longer set apart? If we jump ahead and look at our Bible history, we will find that they once again lost control of their land to the Romans.

Being a people set apart requires obedience. In Ezra's day that was not an easy task, nor is it easy for us. We have many temptations, heartaches, and distractions. But there is also the promise of blessing when we obey. *Whoever has my commands and obeys them, he is the one who loves me. He who loves me will be loved by my Father, and I too will love him and show myself to him* (John 14:21).

MEMORY CHALLENGE

Write out Psalm 37:23 several times as a beginning to memorize it this week.

Appalled

Read Ezra 9:3-5.

1. When Ezra heard the exiles had intermarried with the heathen people around them, what did he do and for how long?

2. Who gathered with Ezra?

3. What do the following scriptures say about trembling at the Word of God?

   Psalm 119:120, 161

   Isaiah 66:2b, 5

4. Ezra was appalled at the sin of the people. They had not trembled at the Word of the Lord, but instead took it lightly. Summarize the following examples of other leaders who were appalled.

   Deuteronomy 9:18-19

   1 Samuel 7:5-6

   2 Samuel 24:10

5. Are we to be appalled at our sin? Summarize the following verses about how we should deal with our sin.

1 Kings 8:33-34

Psalm 32:5

Psalm 51:3-4

1 John 1:8-9

The drama unfolds as Ezra tears his clothes and even pulls hair out of his beard and off his head. He is appalled! How could the people, the holy nation, do such a thing? Yet Ezra's signs of grief gathered those who trembled at the Word of the Lord. His grief served to get the attention of the people concerning the seriousness of sin. They sat there until 2:30-3:30 p.m., the time of the evening offering.

Maybe in those long hours they named their sin. Maybe intermarriage was their only sin, but maybe there was more. But it was a time of soul searching and humbling themselves before the Lord in grief, and naming each sin.

We, too, must name our sins. How can we correct a sin through the help of the Holy Spirit if we do not identify it? If our sin is pride, we must name it and ask the Holy Spirit to make us aware each time pride enters into our day. If our sin is lust, we must recognize that and ask the Holy Spirit to make us sensitive to this sin so we can correct it. If our sin is gossip, we must confess it and ask the Holy Spirit to control our tongues. It is easy to downplay a sin if we do not identify it specifically. We must name it and be appalled that we have lived this way. Only then can we know our personal weakness in sin and with God's help, turn from our sin.

MEMORY CHALLENGE

Whose way does the Lord delight in?

Ashamed

Read Ezra 9:5-7.

1. Why can't Ezra lift up his face to God?

2. What does Ezra say has happened to the children of Israel due to their sins?

3. If the Jews did not follow God's law, it was foretold exactly what would happen to them in Deuteronomy 28:36, 64. Summarize these verses.

4. Compare the beginning of Ezra's prayer (verses 6-7) with Daniel's prayer in Daniel 9:4-11. Write down the similarities.

5. What do the following scriptures teach us about being ashamed and humbling ourselves?

   1 Kings 21:28-29

   2 Kings 22:18-20

   2 Chronicles 33:12-13

Micah 6:8

1 Peter 5:5-6

Have you ever been ashamed of something you have done? Have you ever been ashamed of something your family, church, or business has done? That is the situation in which Ezra found himself when he discovered the people's disobedience to the Law through intermarriage. Ezra was personally guiltless, yet he identified with his people in their sin. When we are not set apart from evil, we become involved in evil. Ezra admitted this and was ashamed.

He used the personal pronoun "I" when he confessed. Ezra 9:5 tells us he prayed on his knees, which was a position of humility, and spread out his hands, meaning he was open and concealing nothing in prayer. Then Ezra began with an expression of shame, being unable to lift up his face.

Ezra surveyed the Jewish history of sin. He acknowledged the long story of failure and transgressions that required God's punishment and the Jews' captivity. He included himself in this, for he was guilty by association.

Yesterday, we studied the importance of naming our sin so we know the exact wrong we are facing. In today's lesson, the emphasis is placed on the fact that we should be ashamed of our sin. We shouldn't rationalize it, deny it, or minimize it, but should humble ourselves before God in brokenness over the evil we have done. May we, like Ezra, be willing to admit when it is appropriate to be ashamed.

MEMORY CHALLENGE

If possible, look up two or three other translations (besides NIV) of Psalm 37:23 and record your favorite one below.

Ablaze

Read Ezra 9:8-9.

1. In the first part of Ezra's prayer, he confessed sin and guilt and admitted that the Jews had been in captivity due to their sin. Summarize in your own words the content of his prayer in verses 8-9.

2. If other translations are available, look up in the last phrase of verse 8, which in the NIV reads, *God gives light to our eyes.* What do you think this means?

3. Let's concentrate on part of the phrase, *light to our eyes.* Look up the following scriptures and record them. To the left of each scripture write a one- or two-word description to which the verse is referring.

   Psalm 32:8

   Psalm 119:130

   Lamentations 3:25

   Habakkuk 3:19

4. The following scriptures refer to *light to the eyes.* Record them.

   Psalm 13:3

   Psalm 19:8

5. In 1 Samuel 14:27-29, Jonathan's eyes brightened. Summarize what happened in this incident.

6. What do you believe Ezra means in the second half of the phrase, *relief in our bondage*? Use Galatians 5:1 to help with this answer.

7. Who is the Light of the world, according to John 8:12?

When *God gives light to our eyes and . . . relief in our bondage,* the whole world is ablaze. Ezra is saying we have greatly sinned and failed God again, but in the midst of it He gives us strength, hope, guidance, encouragement, and insight. Then we have relief in our bondage, for we know the good hand of God is still upon us.

June and Joan were friends in high school. Together they ate lunch at school, went to football games, and shopped. Joan became aware through their times of visiting that June seemed to be searching for something. As a Christian, Joan felt she might know the answer and invited June to church.

June attended faithfully on Sunday mornings and joined in some of the youth activities. Then one Sunday morning, when the invitation was given to receive Christ, June walked down the aisle of that church and knelt at the altar. She invited Christ into her life and received Him as her Savior.

When she looked up from her prayer, her face was *ablaze.* June had been in bondage to her own sin, but her confession brought light to her eyes, for she was free in Christ! She now had hope, strength, and insight; there was reason for her heart to be encouraged! Light and forgiveness had come to her through Christ; this showed in her face, and her life was now *ablaze.*

MEMORY CHALLENGE

How does the Lord feel about the man whose steps He has made firm?

Abominations

Read Ezra 9:10-12.

1. How was the Promised Land that God gave the children of Israel polluted by its people?

2. Detestable practices are abominations to the Lord. Define the word "abomination," using a dictionary or Bible concordance.

3. The following scriptures describe specific sins that are abominable to God. Look each one up and list the sin.

   Deuteronomy 7:25-26

   Deuteronomy 12:31

   Deuteronomy 18:9-13

   2 Chronicles 36:14

4. Because of the abominations of the heathen people of the land, the children of Israel were not to _____ (verse 12).

5. What was God's promise to the people if they did not intermarry?

6. What are our present-day abominations to the Lord? List some of your own ideas and then summarize what the following scriptures say about this.

Luke 16:13-15

Titus 1:15-16

1 Peter 4:3-6

"Things utterly repulsive" is the definition of "abomination," according to *Guideposts Family Concordance*. God had specifically spelled out what these things were to His children, yet they still chose to disobey. Today we don't have to look very far to find our own detestable practices. Most Christians would quickly list child abuse, abortion, pornography, violence, and corruption in leadership, among many other things. Yet we also, like the exiles, have an opportunity to turn from such abominations.

Chuck Colson certainly was an example of a man involved in the detestable practices of his day. Known as Richard Nixon's "hatchet man," who bragged that he would run over his own grandmother to reelect the president, he believed in relative morality. Any means was okay if Colson accomplished his desired end result.

But his life was empty, and somewhere inside, Chuck Colson knew this life of chasing power, influence, status, and money was not what it was all about. When the Watergate problems came to light, Colson's life came tumbling down. In those dark moments, through the influence of Christians around him, he became aware of his own detestable practices. He confessed them and gave his heart over to Christ, and became a changed man.

Chuck Colson organized a powerful prison ministry by the name of Prison Fellowship. He also has given the world several powerful books on salvation, government issues, and Christian principles. He is a wonderful testament to how a life that was an abomination to the Lord can be made clean and turned around to represent Christ.

MEMORY CHALLENGE

Fill in the blanks: "If the LORD _____ in a man's _____, he _____ his _____ firm." Psalm 37:____

Again

Read Ezra 9:13-15.

1. Ezra confessed that what had happened to the children of Israel was a result of their own evil deeds and great guilt. Yet how does he say they were treated by God?

2. Even though "grace" is a New Testament term, is that what Ezra is referring to? How would you define "grace"?

3. Can we cast aside God's grace and expect to survive? Look up Romans 6:1-2 to help with your answer.

4. In this passage, Ezra is agonizing over the possibility that the people will once again cast God's grace aside. Summarize the following two scriptures.

   Deuteronomy 9:8-14

   Psalm 130:3

5. Does Ezra's prayer have any requests in it?

Ezra's prayer has sometimes been called a prayer of penitence. It contains no requests, just the outpourings of a broken heart. A summary of the prayer is as follows:

Ezra 9:5-6	Group guilt admitted
Ezra 9:7	We know better and have received past punishment.
Ezra 9:8-9	Grace greater than all our sins.
Ezra 9:10-14	*Again* we sinned.
Ezra 9:15	*Again* we confess.

God's Riches At Christ's Expense is an acrostic for the word "grace," the great message of God's Word. If we received what we truly deserved, none of us would be saved, but all of us would be destined to eternal damnation. Yet through the mercy of God, He sent His Son, Jesus Christ, as a sacrifice for our sin. We do not have to pay our own debt but instead receive Christ as our Savior and replacement for that sin. He has already paid for the sin through His death on the Cross. All we have to do is receive His grace by faith.

Again, the gift of God is not like the result of the one man's sin: The judgment followed one sin and brought condemnation, but the gift followed many trespasses and brought justification. For if, by the trespass of the one man, death reigned through that one man, how much more will those who receive God's abundant provision of grace and of the gift of righteousness reign in life through the one man, Jesus Christ" (Romans 5:16-17, emphases added).

By entering through faith into what God has always wanted to do for us—set us right with him, make us fit for him—we have it all together with God because of our Master Jesus. And that's not all: We throw open our doors to God and discover at the same moment that he has already thrown open his door to us. We find ourselves standing where we always hoped we might stand—out in the wide open spaces of God's grace and glory, standing tall and shouting our praise (Romans 5:1-5, TM, emphasis added).

Grace, grace, God's grace,
   Grace that will pardon and cleanse within!
Grace, grace, God's grace,
   Grace that is greater than all our sin!
                              —Julia H. Johnston

MEMORY CHALLENGE

Write Psalm 37:23 in this space.

Ezra

■ A study of Ezra 10

Omnipotent Hope

Read Ezra 10, concentrating on verses 1-2.

1. What four things did Ezra do in verse 1?

2. The following scriptures give examples of other leaders showing the people the way. Summarize them.

   Daniel 9:20

   2 Chronicles 20:5-9

3. What was the result of Ezra's actions?

4. Shecaniah came forth as the spokesperson for the people. What was the main idea of his message?

---

5. Give a definition of confession and then summarize the following scriptures.

   Leviticus 5:5

   Joshua 7:19-20

   Matthew 3:5-6

6. What happens when we confess our sins?

   1 Kings 8:33-34

Psalm 37:24

Though he stumble,
he will not fall,
for the LORD upholds him
with his hand.

(NIV)

Psalm 32:3-5

1 John 1:9

7. What role should confession play in our lives?

8. Shecaniah's basic message was that if we confess, we have *hope*. Record the following scriptures regarding *hope*.

   Psalm 42:11

   Psalm 71:5

   Isaiah 49:23

   Jeremiah 29:11

When Ezra prayed, confessed, wept, and threw himself down, the repentant people gathered. Close your eyes to picture the drama and consider how it might draw a crowd. Yet, the people who gathered were not thrill seekers but people who identified with Ezra. They, too, were willing to confess. They wept in sorrow for their sins. Ezra's loving concern for the people encouraged them to repent. Ezra did not accuse, but God convicted the people through his actions.

Then a beautiful thing happened. A man named Shecaniah came forward as a spokesperson. There was nothing special about Shecaniah that we know of. But he led the people powerfully, for he was not willing to keep on sinning. In spite of the sins of the people, he believed there was hope.

Hope is a powerful motivator. Without it we would often give up. But if we have hope, we are able to keep

going and believe that our circumstances can change for the better.

Meredith was a divorced woman who had married a second time. She had custody of her two children from her first marriage. However, when the children were ages 4 and 6, they were kidnapped by their father. Although Meredith tried desperately to locate her children, she was unsuccessful. They were lost to her for several years, until they both ran away from their father. The children called their mother asking to return home.

Meredith felt blessed to have her children back, but she realized she had not had any influence on them during most of the formative years in their lives. As they grew into teenagers, more and more problems developed until Meredith had to take a "tough love" philosophy. She would no longer allow the kids to live at home unless they abided by her house rules. They both left home, each deciding to make his own way in the world.

Meredith's present husband, Jim, told her the kids would never get their lives together. But Meredith refused to believe that. She recognized there was always hope. She kept loving her kids, every once in a while going to where they worked to say hello and give them a hug. There were no encouraging signs at that point, but she believed no situation was ever hopeless.

After a while both kids got tired of the mess their lives were in. They agreed to live by the family rules and moved back home. Presently, both are enrolled in college, working part-time and living somewhat stable lives. There are still problems, but the situation is greatly improved.

What would have happened to the kids if their mother had given up on them? What would have happened if she lost hope? In this case, Meredith was not a believer; even so she had hope. Just think how much more hope we as Christians have in our lives because of God's wonderful promises! Hope is a wonderful motivator, enabling us to keep trying, loving, and setting a godly example. Hope is believing a difficult problem can be solved. Hope is trusting God with every circumstance even when it looks bleak. Hope is refusing to despair because we know confession can bring new life.

MEMORY CHALLENGE

Go back and read the entire memory challenge for the book of Ezra. Be prepared to write this at the end of the week. Read Psalm 37:24 aloud several times, since it is the new verse.

Oath

Read Ezra 10:3-6.

1. What was Shecaniah's plan?

2. Ezra agreed to the plan and made sure the people were committed by requiring an _____.

3. Lip service in confession is not enough. There must be an action step of changed attitude and behavior. By requiring the oath, Ezra was challenging the people to make a commitment and truly repent. Look up the scriptures below, which refer to other action steps, and summarize the situation.

   Genesis 21:8-21

   Acts 5:1-10

   Acts 19:18-19

4. How would taking an oath help us to take an action step?

5. The phrase "send away" in verse 3 means "divorce." Summarize what the following Old Testament passage says about divorce and how Christ responded to that.

   Deuteronomy 24:1

Matthew 19:3-9

After the people had confessed their sin, the required action step was to take an oath to correct the problem. Maybe Shecaniah was the originator of accountability groups, for he realized that confession wasn't enough and that the people needed an oath to bind them to the action step.

Accountability or support groups are not new but are somewhat popular again. The purpose is to support one another while holding each other accountable for a particular behavior. So members of an accountability group for alcoholics, for example, are responsible to help each other to keep from drinking. When a member is sorely tempted to give in and take a drink, he or she is able to call a fellow group member whose role is to talk them out of such action. At each group meeting, each member is expected to report on his own progress.

To be effective, accountability groups must be built on the principles of love, honesty, acceptance, and commitment to each other. Confession is vital when a group member slips back into his previous pattern of behavior. If this is not done, the group cannot help support or confront. Also, when a member lets others know the condition of his heart, it leads to help and trust and helps to head off potential problems. As we learn to overcome life's temptations, it's important for us to share our stories and our answers to prayer.

In order to take part in an accountability group, members generally have to make a commitment and, in a sense, take an "oath" to sincerely work on the issues that tempt them personally, as well as to support and encourage other group members. What a beautiful thing to make an oath to be committed to the ways of God and growing as much as possible in Him!

MEMORY CHALLENGE

Recite Psalm 37:23, last week's verse, to yourself and then answer this question. Who may stumble but not fall because the Lord upholds him with His hand?

Order for the Occasion

Read Ezra 10:7-11.

1. The exiles were ordered to assemble. What was to be their punishment if they did not?

2. Verse 9 tells us the people were greatly distressed for two reasons. What were these?

3. Ezra said to the exiles, "You have been
   _____." Then he named the sin
   again. What was it? _____
   Then he stated they should _____
   and follow up with the action step of _____
   _____
   (verse 11). Finally he mentioned separating
   themselves from the _____ _____ .

4. What does God's Word say about being unfaithful?
   Summarize the following scriptures.

   2 Chronicles 29:6

   Psalm 78:56-57

   Proverbs 25:19

Matthew 25:14-30

5. What is God's promise if we turn from our unfaithfulness?

   Leviticus 26:40-42

   2 Chronicles 34:27

On December 8, 457 B.C., the people assembled in the open space before the Temple as ordered. They came because if they didn't, their property would be confiscated and appropriated for Temple use. This was warning enough for everyone to come.

The people were affected in two ways on this occasion. First, they trembled in fear of God. Remember the exiles did not deny their sins, but confessed. Now they were afraid, for they knew God would not be patient forever, and someday they would face His judgment. Second, their assembling so promptly showed their sense of urgency to correct this sin in spite of the weather. This was the rainy season in Jerusalem and could be cold and miserable. They did hurry to make a decision about how they would proceed so everyone could get out of the rain (verse 13).

The main ideas of Ezra's message concerned unfaithfulness, confession, and doing God's will. Often the Holy Spirit makes us aware of our unfaithfulness and we confess, but then we get confused when we try to determine God's will in the matter. Yet we are promised that if we are faithful, He will reveal to us just what He wants us to do in each situation. May our sincere prayer be *Teach me to do your will, for you are my God* (Psalm 143:10).

MEMORY CHALLENGE

Who does the Lord uphold with His hand?

Officials and Opposition

Read Ezra 10:12-15.

1. The whole assembly admitted to Ezra that he was right. What was the plan they suggested?

2. Were the people following a plan they had followed before in other times of disobedience? Summarize these scriptures from 2 Chronicles.

   2 Chronicles 29:10-11

   2 Chronicles 30:6-9

3. Did anyone oppose this plan? If so, who?

4. Is it appropriate for God-fearing people to sometimes disagree and oppose each other's ideas? What do the following scriptures say about this?

   Matthew 16:21-23

   Acts 15:36-41

5. Opposition in itself can be healthy as long as it is not divisive. Summarize the following scriptures where opposition was a problem.

   Acts 18:6

   1 Timothy 6:20

   2 Timothy 2:25-26

6. What have you learned personally about when it is appropriate to oppose a plan and when it is best to let it go so as not to be divisive? This would be a good topic to share with your group.

The exiles wanted things to be done correctly and in an orderly fashion. So the judges set a time to meet personally with each one involved in intermarriage.

For some reason, four people opposed this plan. We really don't know why. Of these four, none, except possibly Meshullam, was an offender. Elsewhere in the book of Ezra, a man named Meshullam was noted as being guilty of intermarriage, but there are 10 men with this name listed in Ezra and Nehemiah, so there was only a 10% chance this was the same one. So maybe these men opposed the plan simply because they did not like the specific procedure picked. Or maybe they did not want to have the women and children sent away. Maybe they were the type who opposed anything they did not think of themselves. We really don't know.

What we do know is that they chose not to be divisive. They are mentioned in this one verse, and then the matter is dropped. It did not become a problem. They apparently chose to let it go. What a wonderful gift, to know when it is worth taking a stand and when it is better to drop it. The exiles were able to proceed in the face of opposition because they were mature in their faith. This is much like the model we see in Paul and Barnabas who chose to split up, but both continued to work for the Lord. We do not have to be "yes" people, but we do need to learn to recognize when to oppose and when to let it go.

MEMORY CHALLENGE

Can you think of a time when you personally have stumbled but the Lord upheld you with His hand?

Only One

Read Ezra 10:16-17.

1. How long did it take for Ezra and the officials to investigate all the cases?

2. Ezra required separation in each case for two reasons. Each of the following scriptures gives one of the reasons. List them below.

   Leviticus 20:22-24

   Exodus 23:31-33

3. Read 1 Corinthians 7:12-17. Summarize what the New Testament states about living with unbelieving spouses.

4. Why do you think the Old Testament viewpoint about being married to unbelievers is different from the New Testament viewpoint?

5. Would there ever be a situation where a New Testament believer would need to separate himself from an unbelieving spouse? This is an opinion question on which we will not all agree. If possible, back your opinion up with an example or scripture. For additional thought-provoking ideas read Matthew 12:25-30.

6. The exiles gave up individual families in order for the whole community to be blessed by obeying God's command to be a people set apart. Also, the exiles wanted to avoid further discipline through another exile. This foreshadows what one Person did for everyone in the New Testament. Who is this Only One and what did He do? Use the following scriptures to help with your answer.

John 18:14

John 3:16-17

The plan of the exiles was to break up families and send wives and children away. Where would they go? How would they be supported? Didn't God care about them too? We are reminded here of the story of Hagar when Abraham sent her and Ishmael away after Sarah became jealous (Genesis 21:8-21). God allowed Abraham to send the two away, but the Lord also intervened and took care of them.

Just as the exiles had gotten mixed up with the pagans, Susan Atkins, a young teenager, got mixed up with the wrong group. She was searching for truth and love in all the wrong places. By her later teen years, she thought she had found a "family" who had the answers and avidly followed whatever their leader and her boyfriend, Charlie Manson, said to do. This involved illicit sex, widespread drug use, stealing, and eventually murder. In her twisted thinking, Susan believed Charlie Manson's group was opposed to evil people who took advantage of others. She believed the violent methods chosen by the group were justified because they were really doing good. In this "family," she believed she had found what she had been searching for all her life—love, support, friendship, community, excitement, and security.

But her lifestyle eventually led her to death row in prison. There she began to realize she had been fooled, and what she believed to be good was really evil. One day she was introduced to the Only One who gave up His own life so that all of us could be saved from our sins. Susan not only accepted Jesus as her Savior but began to follow Him by studying His Word, praying, and sharing her story with anyone who would listen. She was a changed person with a radiant witness.

Sometimes when we think we have it all figured out, God shows us what we thought was good may not be good at all. Then at great cost we may be asked to turn from our evil. We will suffer consequences, but God also provides His grace. The exiles lost family members. Susan Atkins ended up in prison. But like Hagar, God does not intend to leave His children uncared for. He has a plan for our lives. He provided the Only One to deliver us.

MEMORY CHALLENGE

Fill in the blanks: "Though he _____, _____ _____ _____ _____, for the _____ _____ _____ _____ _____ _____." Psalm 37:_____

Offenders

Read Ezra 10:18-44.

1. Who are the five groups of offenders who married foreign wives?

2. What did the priests offer as a guilt offering (verse 19)?

3. A precedent was already set for the guilt offering. Summarize Leviticus 6:6-7.

4. The exiles who had intermarried admitted they were offenders, but they were willing to do whatever it took to return to God. Hezekiah encouraged his people in the same way through a letter. List the major points of this letter found in 2 Chronicles 30:6-9.

5. The glorious message of Ezra is that even though we may be offenders, we can always return to God and He will graciously deliver us. Summarize the following verses.

   Deuteronomy 4:29-31

2 Chronicles 6:24-25

Isaiah 34:16-17

1 Thessalonians 1:9

A total of 113 Jews were involved in the sin of intermarriage. Seventeen were priests, 10 were Levites, which included the singer and gatekeepers, and 86 were laymen. This means that 25% of the total were religious leaders. Certainly they did not set a very good example when they broke the Law, but their example was good when they recommitted themselves to it.

The forced breakup of these intermarriages was a bitter pill to swallow. Who was going to support these wives and children now that they were going back home? The children would be fatherless. Yet the children were pagans and expressly forbidden from inheriting any of the land, so even if they stayed, life would be difficult. The sins of the fathers were going to be visited on the children (Exodus 20:5). It is a heart-wrenching story.

How could the exiles have avoided these problems? Not all problems can be avoided, for we are told that in this world we will have tribulation (John 16:33). However, when we choose to disobey, we are assured of creating problems. The consequences of our sins will remain in much the same way as the problems created by these intermarriages remained. But the marvelous truth is that we can always, always return to God. Offenders are eligible for grace. Whatever our sin may be, in God we have *hope and a future* (Jeremiah 29:11).

MEMORY CHALLENGE

Write out from memory Psalm 37:1-6, 18-19, and 23-24.